# Make More of Vegetables

## JANET WARREN

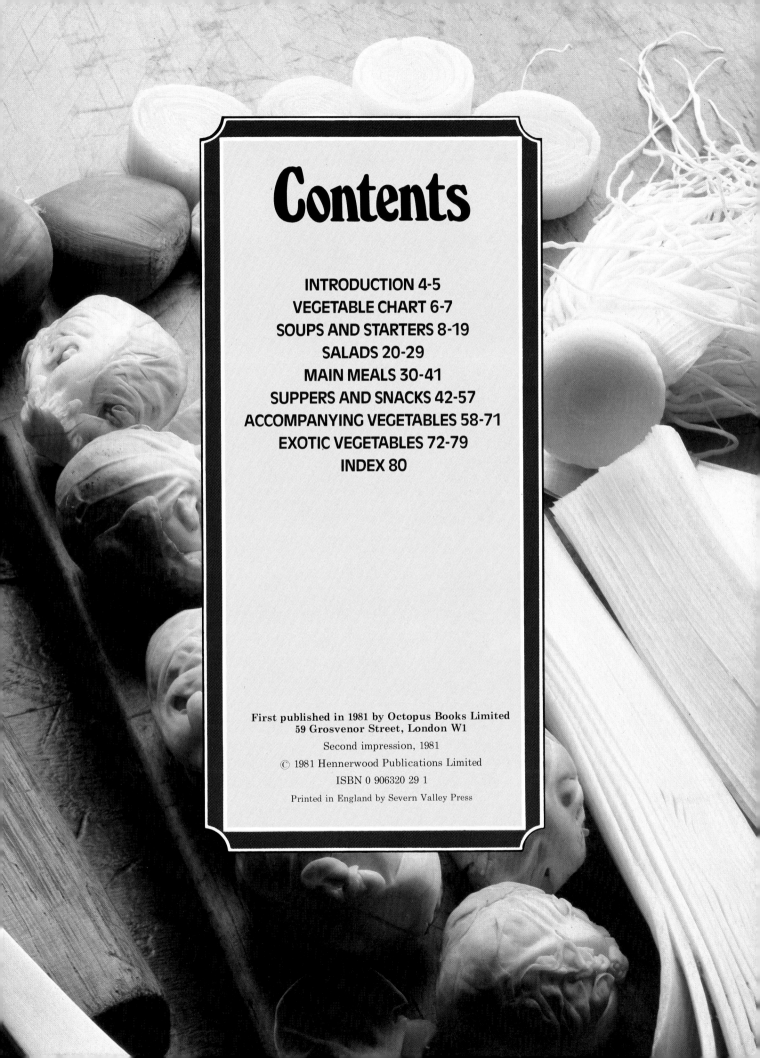

# Contents

First published in 1981 by Octopus Books Limited
59 Grosvenor Street, London W1

Second impression, 1981

© 1981 Hennerwood Publications Limited

ISBN 0 906320 29 1

Printed in England by Severn Valley Press

# INTRODUCTION

Cooking with vegetables has, until recently, been looked upon either as the secondary part of the meal or of real interest only to those people who follow a vegetarian diet.

However, nowadays, with the high cost of other foods and the increased interest in 'grow your own', vegetables are at last receiving the attention they deserve. It is fortunate that not only do we in this country have access to a wonderful array of produce from our own soil but, due to vastly improved travel facilities, we are able to import specialities from all over the world.

As with all fresh produce, vegetables should be used as soon as possible after harvesting or bought from a shop that has a quick turnover. The fresher the vegetable, the better the flavour. Here are a few tips on what to look for when buying vegetables.

**Root vegetables,** e.g. potatoes, carrots, swedes
- Avoid produce covered in earth as it can prove to be a very expensive way of buying soil for the garden.
- Make sure the vegetables are firm and not dull and shrivelled.
- If possible, check the skin of new potatoes. If it can be removed easily with the fingernail, then the potatoes will peel easily.
- Avoid large swedes, they can be woody in the centre.
- If possible, buy parsnips after the first frost as the flavour is much improved.

**Green vegetables,** e.g. cabbage, spring greens
- Choose green vegetables that are bright and strong in colour.
- Avoid any with yellow tinges to the leaves.
- Make sure cabbage has a firm centre.
- Check the stalk end of white cabbage to see if it is woody or starting to soften.

**Salad vegetables,** e.g. lettuce, endive, cucumber
- Always select fresh-looking lettuce. Avoid any that are starting to turn yellow.
- Make sure a lettuce such as a Webb's Wonder has a good heart to it.
- Cos lettuce should not be too large or dark green in colour, as this can mean it is tough.
- If possible, feel the cucumber to ensure it is firm.

**Fruit,** e.g. tomato, marrow, courgette
- Choose tomatoes firm to the touch and preferably with stalks that are not too shrivelled.
- The degree of redness depends slightly on the variety of tomato but make sure they are not under-ripe.
- Buy marrows that have a soft skin. The fingernail should penetrate the surface easily.
- Avoid large courgettes and buy ones that have a bright and shiny skin.

**Flower,** e.g. broccoli, cauliflower, Brussels sprouts
- The flower head on cauliflowers should be white, firm and unblemished.
- Broccoli spears should be either green or purple in colour. Avoid any that are turning yellow.
- Select Brussels sprouts that are firm, small and a good colour.

**Dried,** e.g. haricot beans, chick peas
- Choose beans that are not damaged.
- Make sure the packet doesn't contain any dust, etc.
- Buy from a store that has a good turnover as dried vegetables keep for only about 6 months, after which time they are almost impossible to cook to a soft texture.

Brussels sprouts with chestnuts; Stuffed cabbage leaves

| Vegetable | Preparation | Cooking | Amount to allow and serving suggestion |
|---|---|---|---|
| **Artichoke, Globe** Available all year | Trim and soak for 15 mins in salted cold water. | Boil in salted water for about 30 mins. Drain. | Allow 1 per person. Serve hot with hollandaise sauce or melted butter and lemon juice, or cold with vinaigrette. |
| **Artichoke, Jerusalem** Available November to May | Scrub, peel and cover in water with a little lemon juice added. | Cook in boiling, salted water with lemon juice for 30 mins, or slice and fry in equal quantities of butter and oil. | Allow 175–225 g/6–8 oz per person. Toss in melted butter or coat with a white or cheese sauce. |
| **Asparagus** | see page 14 | see page 14 | see page 14 |
| **Aubergine (egg plant)** Available all year | Cut into 1 cm/½ inch slices. Lay on a plate, sprinkle with salt and leave for 30 mins to draw off some of the excess liquid. Rinse and dry. | Fry in equal quantities of butter and oil or coat in flour and deep fry. | Allow 175 g/6 oz per person. Serve as an accompanying vegetable or halved and stuffed for a supper dish. |
| **Beans, French** Available all year | Top and tail and keep whole if not too large. | Cook in boiling, salted water for 15 mins. Drain. | Allow 100–225 g/4–8 oz per person. Serve hot tossed in butter or cold in a salad. |
| **Beans, Runner** Available July to October | Top, tail, string and slice. | Cook in boiling, salted water for 15 mins. Drain. | Allow 100–225 g/4–8 oz per person. Serve hot tossed in butter or cold in a salad. |
| **Beetroot** Available all year round | Twist off and discard the leaves. Wash thoroughly. | Cook in boiling water until tender – about 2 hours depending on size. Peel and slice. | Allow 100–150 g/4–6 oz per person. Serve cold either sliced or diced with a dressing or hot, coated in a white sauce. |
| **Broad Beans** Available April to August | Remove the beans from the shells. | Cook in boiling, salted water for 20–30 mins. | Allow 225 g/8 oz per person. Serve tossed in butter or coat with a parsley sauce. |
| **Broccoli Purple** Available February to May | Discard the coarse outer leaves and stems. Cut the larger heads in half. Wash thoroughly in salted water. Occasionally, stems may be tough, if so, pare them. | Cook in boiling, salted water for 15–20 mins. Drain. | Allow 175–225 g/6–8 oz per person. Serve coated with melted butter and sprinkled with toasted almonds or coat with a hollandaise sauce. |
| **Broccoli, Calabrese (green)** Available June to May | Discard the coarse outer leaves and stems. Cut the larger heads in half. Wash thoroughly in salted water. Occasionally, stems may be tough, if so, pare them. | Cook in boiling, salted water for 15–20 mins. Drain. | Allow 175–225 g/6–8 oz per person. Serve coated with melted butter and sprinkled with toasted almonds or coat with a hollandaise sauce. |
| **Brussels Sprouts** Available September to April | Wash. Remove any damaged leaves. Trim away stalk and cut a small cross in the base if large. | Cook in boiling, salted water for 15 mins. Drain. | Allow 100–150 g/4–6 oz per person. Toss in melted butter, or purée with an equal amount of boiled potatoes. |
| **Cabbage** (Dutch, savoy, red) Available all year | Discard coarse outer leaves. Cut into 4. Remove centre stalk and shred, finely if the cabbage is for a salad. | Cook in boiling, salted water for 10–15 mins. Drain well. Add 1 × 15 ml spoon/1 tablespoon vinegar to water when cookng red cabbage. | Allow 100 g/4 oz per person. Toss in butter with a little grated nutmeg. |
| **Carrots** Available all year | **New:** trim off leaves, then scrape with a knife. **Old:** peel thinly and slice or dice. | **New:** cook in boiling, salted water for 15 mins. **Old:** cook in boiling, salted water for 20 mins. Drain well. | Allow 100–150 g/4–6 oz per person. Toss in butter with chopped parsley or chives. |
| **Cauliflower** Available all year, best from June to October | Trim off the tops of the stalks and the base and cut a cross in the base to enable the water to penetrate right into the vegetable. Can also be broken into pieces – florets. | Place flower uppermost in boiling, salted water. Cook for 15–30 mins depending on size. Drain. Cook florets for about 15 mins. | A medium cauliflower will serve 4. Coat with a white or cheese sauce and sprinkle with paprika pepper or sprinkle with breadcrumbs fried in butter. |
| **Celery** Available all year | Trim, wash and scrub thoroughly. Cut into even lengths. | Boil in salted water for 30–40 mins or braise. Parboil for 5 mins, drain and cook in ovenproof dish with butter 180°C, 350°F, Gas mark 4 for 1–1½ hours. | Allow 2–3 sticks per person. Coat boiled celery with a white or herb sauce. |
| **Chicory** (known as endive in France and USA) September to June | Trim off any damaged leaves and with a sharp, pointed knife remove the core. Wash. | Cook in salted water with a little lemon juice for about 15–20 mins. Drain. | Allow 1–2 heads per person when cooked, less in a salad. Serve tossed in butter or coated with a white or cheese sauce. |
| **Courgette (zucchini)** Available all year | Trim off and discard stalks. Wash but don't peel. Either leave whole or slice. Sprinkle slices with salt and leave for 10 mins. Rinse and dry. | Cook whole courgettes in oven with a little butter 180°C, 350°F, Gas mark 4 for 30–40 mins, or slice and fry in equal quantities of butter and oil. | Allow 100 g/4 oz per person. Serve as is. Courgettes can also be halved and stuffed, or sliced and served raw in a salad. |

| Vegetable | Preparation | Cooking | Amount to allow and serving suggestion |
|---|---|---|---|
| **Cucumber**<br>Available all year | Peel and cut into large dice. | Fry in 25 g/1 oz butter for 1 min then cover and sauté for 20 mins until soft. Season after cooking. | Allow 100 g/4 oz per person. Serve either raw in a salad or cooked. |
| **Greens (spring)**<br>Available February to June | Cut off the base. Separate the leaves, remove any coarse stalks, then shred the leaves. | Cook in boiling, salted water, uncovered, for 10–15 mins. Drain thoroughly. | Allow 175–225 g/6–8 oz per person. Serve tossed in butter, with a little nutmeg. |
| **Leeks**<br>Available August to May | Trim off the roots, outer damaged leaves and as much of the green top as necessary. Split to within 2.5 cm/1 inch of base and run under cold water to remove any grit. | Cook in boiling, salted water for 20–30 mins or until tender. Drain thoroughly. Or braise in a little butter in the oven 180°C, 350°F, Gas Mark 4 for 1–1½ hours. | Allow 225 g/8 oz per person. Serve boiled leeks coated with a white or cheese sauce. Or serve cold in a vinaigrette or piquant tomato sauce. |
| **Marrow**<br>Available July to October | Peel, cut into 5 cm/2 inch slices and remove seeds. | Boil in salted water for 15 mins. Drain well. Steam chunks for about 20 mins. | Allow 175 g/6 oz per person. Serve coated with a white sauce, sprinkled with paprika. Marrow can also be stuffed and baked. |
| **Mushrooms**<br>Available all year | Wipe caps and trim stalks. If they are cultivated, there is no need to peel. | Fry sliced or whole in a little melted butter with lemon juice for about 10 mins or until tender. Can also be grilled, or covered in breadcrumbs and fried. | Allow 50 g/2 oz per person. Sprinkle with chopped parsley, if liked. Can be stuffed and served as a first course, or sliced and served raw in a salad. |
| **Onions**<br>Available all year | Peel off and discard outer skin. Slice or chop. | Fry slices in shallow fat for 10–15 mins. Or dip in milk and flour and deep fry for 3–5 mins. Can be boiled whole in salted water for 30–40 mins, or parboiled and baked whole with a roast joint. | Allow 100–150 g/4–6 oz per person. If boiled, serve coated in a white or cheese sauce. |
| **Onions, Spring**<br>Available in summer | Trim off base and discard any damaged leaves. | | Serve raw in a salad. |
| **Parsnips**<br>Available September to May | Peel and cut into chunks. | Cook in boiling, salted water for 30–40 mins or roast. | Allow 175 g/6 oz per person. If boiled, serve tossed in butter. |
| **Peas**<br>Available March to December | Shell and wash. | Cook in boiling, salted water with a sprig of mint for 15 mins. Drain. Braise with shredded lettuce, chopped onion and mint in butter for 15–20 mins. | Allow 225 g/8 oz per person. Toss in melted butter. |
| **Potatoes**<br>Available all year | **Old:** Peel, if to be boiled, roasted, deep- or shallow-fried. Scrub well but do not peel if to be baked.<br>**New:** Leave new potatoes with skins on for fuller flavour. | **Old:** Boil for 30 mins in salted water. Roast around the joint. Fry as chips in hot fat for 10 mins or until tender and crispy. Bake in their jackets 200°C, 400°F, Gas Mark 6 for 1–1½ hours.<br>**New:** Boil for 15–20 mins in salted water or bake wrapped in greaseproof paper with butter and mint for 45 mins–1 hour. | Allow 175 g/6 oz per person. Serve tossed in butter with chopped parsley, if boiled. Split and topped with butter if baked in their jackets. |
| **Spinach**<br>Available all year | Wash well to remove grit and pull off the coarse stems. | Place in pan with no extra water. Add salt and cook for about 10 mins. Drain well. Chop if liked. | Allow 225 g/8 oz per person. Serve tossed in butter or a little single cream. Add raw leaves to a green salad. |
| **Swedes**<br>Available September to June | Peel and cut into even chunks. | Cook in boiling, salted water. Drain and mash, if liked. | Allow 100–150 g/4–6 oz per person. Serve tossed in butter, or mix butter and nutmeg into mashed swede. |
| **Sweet Peppers**<br>Available all year | Cut in half, remove core and all the seeds then chop or slice. | Blanch in boiling water for 1 min and cool, if added to salad. | Allow 100 g/4 oz per person. Serve as part of a casserole, stew or accompanying vegetable, e.g. ratatouille. Or serve stuffed with a savoury mixture. |
| **Sweetcorn**<br>Available February to May and June to November | Remove the outer leaves and thread-like strands inside. | Cook in boiling water, covered, for 20–30 mins. Add salt just before cobs are ready. Drain. | Serve with melted butter. |
| **Tomatoes**<br>Available all year | Wipe and remove green calyx if necessary. | Can be grilled, fried, plain baked or stuffed, or eaten raw. To bake, place in ovenproof dish, cut a cross in the top, dot with butter, cover and cook at 180°C, 350°C, Gas Mark 4 for 30–45 mins. | Allow 1–2 per person. Sprinkle with chopped parsley or basil. Or cut in half, scoop out the centre and serve stuffed with a savoury mixture. |
| **Turnip**<br>Available all year | Peel and, if large, cut into even chunks. | Boil in salted water for 30 mins until tender. Drain. | Allow 100–150 g/4–6 oz per person. Serve tossed in melted butter or mashed with nutmeg. |

# SOUPS AND STARTERS

The first course of a meal is designed to stimulate the appetite. Vegetables, whether in a soup or served on their own such as asparagus, are an excellent choice for this as they are neither too rich nor too filling. Always choose the recipe carefully, bearing in mind it should make a pleasant contrast in flavour and texture to the following courses, and present them attractively. Don't forget when preparing soups, to cut the pieces of vegetable fairly small so that as much flavour as possible is extracted, and season them carefully.

# Watercress soup

| Metric | Imperial |
|---|---|
| 2 bunches watercress | 2 bunches watercress |
| 1 large onion, peeled and chopped | 1 large onion, peeled and chopped |
| 1 large potato, peeled and diced | 1 large potato, peeled and diced |
| 25 g butter or margarine | 1 oz butter or margarine |
| 600 ml chicken stock | 1 pint chicken stock |
| 300 ml milk | ½ pint milk |
| salt | salt |
| freshly ground black pepper | freshly ground black pepper |

Preparation time: 15 minutes
Cooking time: 30 minutes

Wash the watercress thoroughly, removing any coarse stalks. Leave it to drain.
Melt the fat in a large pan, add the onion and potato and cook gently for about 5 minutes or until they start to soften. Stir in half the watercress with the stock and milk. Add plenty of salt and pepper and bring slowly to the boil. Cover and simmer for 20 minutes.
Purée the soup in a liquidizer or rub through a sieve, then return it to the pan. Chop the remaining watercress finely, and stir it into the soup. Serve hot.

# Chilled cucumber soup

| Metric | Imperial |
|---|---|
| 1 large cucumber, peeled | 1 large cucumber, peeled |
| 1 large garlic clove, peeled and crushed | 1 large garlic clove, peeled and crushed |
| 2 × 15 ml spoons distilled vinegar | 2 tablespoons distilled vinegar |
| large handful of mint leaves, chopped | large handful of mint leaves, chopped |
| 300 ml soured cream | ½ pint soured cream |
| 1 × 5 ml spoon caster sugar | 1 teaspoon caster sugar |
| salt | salt |
| freshly ground black pepper | freshly ground black pepper |
| milk or single cream, to finish | milk or single cream, to finish |

Preparation time: 10 minutes (plus chilling)

Accompany this refreshing cold soup with melba toast.

Either liquidize or finely grate the cucumber into a bowl. If using the liquidizer, it may be necessary to add the vinegar at this stage.
Stir in the garlic with the mint, soured cream, caster sugar and salt and pepper to taste. Chill the soup for at least 2 hours before serving. If preferred, stir in a little milk or single cream to make a thinner consistency.
Serve the soup in chilled bowls and garnish each portion with a small sprig of mint.
Serves 4–6

Watercress soup; Chilled cucumber soup

# Cream of artichoke soup

| Metric | Imperial |
| --- | --- |
| 50 g butter or margarine | 2 oz butter or margarine |
| 750 g Jerusalem artichokes, peeled and chopped | 1½ lb Jerusalem artichokes, peeled and chopped |
| 175 g potatoes, peeled and chopped | 6 oz potatoes, peeled and chopped |
| 1 medium onion, peeled and chopped | 1 medium onion, peeled and chopped |
| 600 ml chicken stock | 1 pint chicken stock |
| 300 ml milk | ½ pint milk |
| salt | salt |
| freshly ground black pepper | freshly ground black pepper |
| 150 ml single cream | ¼ pint single cream |
| little paprika pepper | little paprika pepper |

Preparation time: 15 minutes
Cooking time: 40 minutes

When preparing artichokes, always keep them covered with cold water which contains lemon juice so that the vegetables do not discolour.

Melt the fat in a large pan. Stir in the vegetables and cook over a gentle heat until they start to soften but not brown. Pour in the stock and milk and bring to the boil. Cover and simmer for about 35–40 minutes, or until the vegetables are tender.
Purée the soup in a liquidizer or rub through a sieve, then pour it back into the rinsed out pan. Stir in half the cream, taste and adjust the seasoning. Reheat gently, making sure it does not boil.
Divide the soup between bowls, swirl a spoonful of the remaining cream on to the surface and sprinkle with paprika pepper.

# Tomato and orange soup

| Metric | Imperial |
| --- | --- |
| 25 g butter or margarine | 1 oz butter or margarine |
| 750 g tomatoes, chopped | 1½ lb tomatoes, chopped |
| 100 g red lentils | 4 oz red lentils |
| 1 medium carrot, peeled and chopped | 1 medium carrot, peeled and chopped |
| 1 large onion, peeled and chopped | 1 large onion, peeled and chopped |
| 1 orange | 1 orange |
| 1 bay leaf | 1 bay leaf |
| 900 ml chicken stock | 1½ pints chicken stock |
| salt | salt |
| freshly ground black pepper | freshly ground black pepper |

Preparation time: 15 minutes
Cooking time: 1 hour 5 minutes

Heat the fat in a large pan. Add the lentils, carrot and onion and cook over a gentle heat for 5 minutes, stirring occasionally.
Using a potato peeler, pare the rind off the orange and add it to the pan with the tomatoes and bay leaf. Pour in the stock, add salt and pepper, then bring to the boil. Cover and simmer for 1 hour or until all the ingredients are soft.
Remove the bay leaf, then purée the soup in a liquidizer or rub through a sieve twice to give a really smooth texture. Stir in the juice from the orange, taste and adjust the seasoning and serve hot.

**Variation:**
Chill the soup for at least 2 hours, then add a little extra stock if necessary before serving.

Cream of artichoke soup; Tomato and orange soup; Winter soup with sherry

# Winter soup with sherry

| *Metric* | *Imperial* |
|---|---|
| *50 g butter* | *2 oz butter* |
| *225 g swede, peeled and thinly shredded* | *8 oz swede, peeled and thinly shredded* |
| *225 g parsnip, peeled and finely diced* | *8 oz parsnip, peeled and finely diced* |
| *100 g turnip, peeled and grated* | *4 oz turnip, peeled and grated* |
| *¼ × 5 ml spoon ground turmeric* | *¼ teaspoon ground turmeric* |
| *1 × 5 ml spoon curry powder* | *1 teaspoon curry powder* |
| *1.2 litres chicken stock* | *2 pints chicken stock* |
| *3 × 15 ml spoons sherry* | *3 tablespoons sherry* |
| *salt* | *salt* |
| *freshly ground black pepper* | *freshly ground black pepper* |
| *3 × 15 ml spoons chopped fresh parsley* | *3 tablespoons chopped fresh parsley* |

Preparation time: 10 minutes
Cooking time: 35 minutes

Melt the butter in a large saucepan. Add the swede, parsnip and turnip, cover and fry gently for about 10 minutes until beginning to soften.
Stir in the turmeric and curry powder, then pour in the stock and bring to the boil. Cover and simmer for 20 minutes until the vegetables are completely soft.
Stir in the sherry and add salt and pepper to taste. Turn into a soup tureen and sprinkle the parsley over the surface. Serve hot with warm brown bread.
Serves 4–6

# Borsch

| Metric | Imperial |
|---|---|
| 1.75 litres chicken or beef stock | 3 pints chicken or beef stock |
| 100 g white cabbage, finely shredded and chopped | 4 oz white cabbage, finely shredded and chopped |
| 1 carrot, peeled and finely chopped | 1 carrot, peeled and finely chopped |
| 1 onion, peeled and finely chopped | 1 onion, peeled and finely chopped |
| 1 celery stick, finely chopped | 1 celery stick, finely chopped |
| 450 g raw beetroot, peeled | 1 lb raw beetroot, peeled |
| 1 × 15 ml spoon chopped fresh parsley | 1 tablespoon chopped fresh parsley |
| 2 cloves | 2 cloves |
| 1 bay leaf | 1 bay leaf |
| 2 tomatoes, peeled, seeded and chopped | 2 tomatoes, peeled, seeded and chopped |
| 2 × 5 ml spoons caster sugar | 2 teaspoons caster sugar |
| juice of 1/2 lemon | juice of 1/2 lemon |
| salt | salt |
| freshly ground black pepper | freshly ground black pepper |
| 150 ml soured cream | 1/4 pint soured cream |

Preparation time: 20 minutes
Cooking time: 1 hour

This traditional Russian soup should be thick with vegetables but don't forget they must be cut small so that they fit easily on to a soup spoon. If you have a liquidizer, you will find the task of preparing the beetroot much cleaner by placing it into the goblet, a little at a time, with some of the stock and quickly chopping it to size. Alternatively, the beetroot can be coarsely grated. Borsch makes an ideal soup to serve to a large number of guests.

Put the stock into a large pan with the cabbage, carrot, onion and celery. Prepare the beetroot and add three-quarters to the stock with the parsley, cloves and bay leaf. Bring to the boil, then cover and simmer for 30 minutes.
Add the tomatoes, sugar, lemon juice, salt and pepper and simmer for a further 20 minutes. To ensure the soup is a good red colour, stir in the remaining beetroot, then simmer for a further 10 minutes. Serve hot with a spoonful of soured cream in each bowl.
Serves 8–10

Borsch; Gazpacho; Leek and potato soup

# Gazpacho

| Metric | Imperial |
|---|---|
| 50 g fresh white breadcrumbs | 2 oz fresh white breadcrumbs |
| 3 × 15 ml spoons distilled malt vinegar | 3 tablespoons distilled malt vinegar |
| 350 ml tomato juice, chilled | 12 fl oz tomato juice, chilled |
| 300 ml cold water, chilled | 1/2 pint cold water chilled |
| 100 g tomatoes, roughly chopped | 4 oz tomatoes, roughly chopped |
| 1/4 cucumber, peeled and roughly chopped | 1/4 cucumber, peeled and roughly chopped |
| 1 small green pepper, cored, seeded and chopped | 1 small green pepper, cored, seeded and chopped |
| 100 g onions, peeled and chopped | 4 oz onions, peeled and chopped |
| 1 garlic clove, peeled and crushed | 1 garlic clove, peeled and crushed |
| 4 × 15 ml spoons olive oil | 4 tablespoons olive oil |
| crushed ice | crushed ice |

Preparation time: 20 minutes

This delicious cold Spanish soup should be served with separate bowls of chopped tomatoes, cucumber, green pepper and fried croûtons of bread to sprinkle over the soup before eating.

Soak the bread in the vinegar. Mix the tomatoes, cucumber, pepper, onions and garlic together, then purée them in a liquidizer or put through a fine mincer. Strain the mixture into a bowl. Mix in the breadcrumb mixture and gradually stir in the oil, drop by drop. Stir in the chilled tomato juice and water, then taste and adjust the seasoning.
Stir the crushed ice into the soup just before serving.
Serves 5–6

# Leek and potato soup

**Metric**
75 g butter or margarine
750 g leeks, trimmed and
cut into 1 cm lengths
225 g potatoes, peeled
and chopped
1 medium onion, peeled
and chopped
900 ml chicken stock
salt
freshly ground black
pepper
300 ml milk
2–3 × 15 ml spoons single
cream
few chopped fresh chives

**Imperial**
3 oz butter or margarine
1½ lb leeks, trimmed and
cut into ½ inch lengths
8 oz potatoes, peeled
and chopped
1 medium onion, peeled
and chopped
1½ pints chicken stock
salt
freshly ground black
pepper
½ pint milk
2–3 tablespoons single
cream
few chopped fresh chives

Preparation time: 20 minutes
Cooking time: 45 minutes

Melt the fat in a large pan. Add the leeks and cook slowly over a low heat for 10 minutes, stirring occasionally. Add the potatoes and onion and cook slowly for a few more minutes. Pour in the stock and add salt and pepper. Cover and simmer for about 30 minutes, or until all the vegetables are soft.

Purée the soup in a liquidizer or rub through a sieve twice to give a really smooth texture. Bring it back to the boil.

Swirl a little of the cream on to the top of each serving and sprinkle with a few chopped chives. Serve with melba toast.

Serves 6

**Variation:**
For a Vichyssoise, chill the soup thoroughly when puréed, then stir in almost 150 ml/¼ pint single cream, leaving a few spoonfuls for decoration.

# Fresh asparagus with butter

| Metric | Imperial |
|--------|----------|
| 450 g asparagus | 1 lb asparagus |
| salt | salt |
| 100 g butter, melted | 4 oz butter, melted |

Preparation time: 10 minutes
Cooking time: 15 minutes

Use a wide, not too shallow pan to cook the asparagus in. A fish fryer with wire basket or an electric frying pan is ideal.

Wash the asparagus stalks thoroughly under cold, running water, taking care not to damage the delicate tops. Trim off the bases, cutting all the stalks to the same lengths. Grade them if necessary. Tie the spears into two bundles so that they can be easily lifted.
Lay the asparagus in the bottom of the pan and pour over enough boiling water to cover. Add salt and simmer for about 15 minutes until tender, the time depends on the size of the stalks.
Drain the asparagus well, untie them, then serve with the melted butter or one of the other suggested sauces.
Serves 3–4

### Variation:

Mix 1 finely chopped hard-boiled egg and 1 × 15 ml spoon/1 tablespoon chopped fresh parsley into the melted butter before serving.

# Globe artichokes with butter

| Metric | Imperial |
|--------|----------|
| 4 globe artichokes | 4 globe artichokes |
| lemon juice or vinegar | lemon juice or vinegar |
| 100 g butter, melted | 4 oz butter, melted |
| salt | salt |

Preparation time: 10 minutes
Cooking time: 30–40 minutes

Serve the artichokes either hot or cold with one of the various sauces suggested.

Trim off the long stalks from the artichokes. If the artichokes are dusty, soak them for up to an hour in cold, salted water. Rinse, then prepare for cooking.
Strip away the tough outer leaves of the artichoke and cut off about 1 cm/½ inch from the top. Snip off the tops of all the leaves around the sides.
Using a small, sharp-edged spoon, scrape out and discard the tender cone of leaves in the centre called the 'choke', making sure every piece of fibre is removed. Keep the prepared artichokes in a bowl of cold water with lemon juice or vinegar so that they do not discolour.
Bring a large pan of salted water to the boil, add lemon juice or vinegar, then cook the artichokes for 30–40 minutes or until a leaf will pull away easily. Drain the artichokes upside down for a few minutes then serve with the butter, and finger bowls of warm water.
To eat an artichoke, strip away a leaf, then, holding it in the fingers, dip it into the selected sauce. Draw it lightly through your teeth to remove the tender part and leave the inedible piece on the side of your plate. Continue in this way until you reach the heart of the artichoke, scrape away the choke if it has not already been removed and eat the heart with a knife and fork.

# Hollandaise sauce

| Metric | Imperial |
|---|---|
| 3 × 15 ml spoons wine vinegar | 3 tablespoons wine vinegar |
| 6 peppercorns | 6 peppercorns |
| 1 small bay leaf | 1 small bay leaf |
| 2 × 15 ml spoons water | 2 tablespoons water |
| 3 egg yolks | 3 egg yolks |
| 175 g butter, melted and cooled | 6 oz butter, melted and cooled |
| salt | salt |
| lemon juice | lemon juice |

Preparation time: 5 minutes
Cooking time: 10 minutes

Serve this rich buttery sauce instead of melted butter with the fresh asparagus.

Put the vinegar, peppercorns and bay leaf into a pan and boil rapidly until the liquid is reduced to a third. Strain and discard the bay leaf and peppercorns. Return the liquid to the pan, add the water with the egg yolks and mix well with a wire whisk until frothy. Beat the mixture continuously over a gentle heat until it is mousse-like. Gradually beat in the melted butter to make a thick sauce. Add salt and a little lemon juice to taste, then keep warm in a bowl over a pan of hot water until required.

# Sauce tartare

| Metric | Imperial |
|---|---|
| 150 ml mayonnaise | ¼ pint mayonnaise |
| 1 × 5 ml spoon chopped fresh parsley | 1 teaspoon chopped fresh parsley |
| 1 × 5 ml spoon chopped fresh tarragon | 1 teaspoon chopped fresh tarragon |
| 1 × 5 ml spoon chopped gherkins | 1 teaspoon chopped gherkins |
| 1 × 5 ml spoon chopped capers | 1 teaspoon chopped capers |

Preparation time: 5 minutes

Beat the parsley, tarragon, gherkins and capers into the mayonnaise and serve with the cold cooked artichokes.

Fresh asparagus with butter; Globe artichokes with butter; Hollandaise sauce; Sauce tartare

# Corn on the cob with sweet and sour sauce

| Metric | Imperial |
|---|---|
| 50 g dried apricots, chopped and soaked overnight in cold water | 2 oz dried apricots, chopped and soaked overnight in cold water |
| 1 small green pepper, seeded and chopped | 1 small green pepper, seeded and chopped |
| 1 small onion, peeled and chopped | 1 small onion, peeled and chopped |
| 2 celery sticks, chopped | 2 celery sticks, chopped |
| 150 ml malt vinegar | 1/4 pint malt vinegar |
| 4 × 15 ml spoons demerara sugar | 4 tablespoons demerara sugar |
| 2 × 15 ml spoons tomato ketchup | 2 tablespoons tomato ketchup |
| 1 × 15 ml spoon cornflour | 1 tablespoon cornflour |
| 4 corn on the cob, trimmed | 4 corn on the cob, trimmed |
| salt | salt |

Preparation time: 10 minutes
Cooking time: 30 minutes

Drain the apricots, and put them in a pan with the pepper, onion and celery. Cover with cold water and bring to the boil. Simmer for 20–30 minutes until the vegetables are soft. Strain, reserving the cooking liquid.

Put the vinegar, sugar and ketchup into a pan. Blend the cornflour with some of the reserved liquid to make a smooth, thin paste. Pour this into the vinegar mixture and bring to the boil, stirring until thickened. Purée the vegetables and stir them into the sauce, then taste and adjust the seasoning.

Cover and cook the corn on the cobs in boiling water for 20 minutes, or until tender, adding salt only for the last 5 minutes of the cooking time. Drain the cobs well and serve on a warm plate with a little of the hot sauce poured over each and the rest served separately.

# Continental courgettes

| Metric | Imperial |
|---|---|
| 4 small courgettes (about 350 g), trimmed | 4 small courgettes (about 12 oz), trimmed |
| grated rind and juice of 1/2 lemon | grated rind and juice of 1/2 lemon |
| salt | salt |
| 1 × 15 ml spoon salad oil | 1 tablespoon salad oil |
| 1 hard-boiled egg, chopped | 1 hard-boiled egg, chopped |
| 2 × 15 ml spoons cottage cheese | 2 tablespoons cottage cheese |
| 2 × 15 ml spoons coarsely chopped fresh mint | 2 tablespoons coarsely chopped fresh mint |
| 25 g walnuts, chopped | 1 oz walnuts, chopped |
| pinch of paprika pepper | pinch of paprika pepper |

| **To garnish:** | **To garnish:** |
|---|---|
| lemon twists | lemon twists |
| few mint leaves | few mint leaves |
| lettuce leaves | lettuce leaves |

Preparation time: 20 minutes
Cooking time: 5 minutes

Cook the whole courgettes in boiling, salted water for 5 minutes, then drain well. Cut the courgettes in half lengthwise and scoop out a channel in the centre using a teaspoon. Finely chop the scooped out flesh and set aside in a bowl.

Put the lemon rind and juice into a bowl, mix in the oil, then add the courgette shells. Leave them to marinate in the mixture until quite cold.

Stir the chopped egg into the chopped courgette flesh with the cottage cheese, mint, walnuts, paprika pepper, salt, pepper and a little of the marinade to moisten. Arrange two courgette shells on a bed of lettuce on each serving plate. Pile the egg mixture into the centre of the courgettes, then garnish each serving with a lemon twist and mint leaf. Serve with thinly sliced brown bread.

Corn on the cob with sweet and sour sauce; Ratatouille; Continental courgettes

# Ratatouille

**Preparation time:** 20 minutes
**Cooking time:** 2 hours
**Oven:** 160°C, 325°F, Gas Mark 3

| Metric | Imperial |
|---|---|
| *1 medium aubergine, sliced* | *1 medium aubergine, sliced* |
| *salt* | *salt* |
| *4–6 × 15 ml spoons oil* | *4–6 tablespoons oil* |
| *450 g tomatoes, peeled and quartered* | *1 lb tomatoes, peeled and quartered* |
| *1 green pepper, cored, seeded and sliced* | *1 green pepper, cored, seeded and sliced* |
| *450 g courgettes, sliced* | *1 lb courgettes, sliced* |
| *350 g onions, peeled and sliced* | *12 oz onions, peeled and sliced* |
| *1 large garlic clove, peeled and crushed* | *1 large garlic clove, peeled and crushed* |
| *pinch of caster sugar* | *pinch of caster sugar* |
| *freshly ground black pepper* | *freshly ground black pepper* |
| *1 bay leaf* | *1 bay leaf* |

Ratatouille is served hot or cold as a first course, thickly sprinkled with Parmesan cheese, or as an accompanying vegetable to grilled meat.

Sprinkle the aubergine slices generously with salt and leave for 20 minutes to draw out the excess moisture. Rinse, drain and pat dry.

Heat the oil in a large frying pan. Mix the aubergine with the tomatoes, pepper, courgettes and garlic. Add them to the oil in batches if necessary and fry for about 8 minutes, turning occasionally.

Transfer the mixture to a 1.75 litre/3 pint casserole dish. Stir in the sugar and plenty of pepper. Add the bay leaf, cover and cook in a preheated oven for 1½–2 hours or until the vegetables are soft.

# Hummus

**Metric**
225 g chick peas, soaked
   overnight and drained
1 onion, peeled and
   roughly chopped
1 bay leaf
juice of 1 lemon
2 garlic cloves, peeled
   and crushed
2 × 15 ml spoons olive
   oil
300 ml plain unsweetened
   yogurt
1 × 2.5 ml spoon ground
   cumin seed
salt

**To garnish:**
chopped fresh parsley
black olives

**Imperial**
8 oz chick peas, soaked
   overnight and drained
1 onion, peeled and
   roughly chopped
1 bay leaf
juice of 1 lemon
2 garlic cloves, peeled
   and crushed
2 tablespoons olive
   oil
10 fl oz plain
   unsweetened yogurt
½ teaspoon ground cumin
   seed
salt

**To garnish:**
chopped fresh parsley
black olives

Preparation time: 10 minutes
Cooking time: 1–1½ hours

It is best to cook pulses, such as chick peas, without using salt as it tends to toughen them if added at the beginning of the cooking time. Hummus is best made at least 24 hours in advance because it thickens on keeping.

Put the peas into a pan, cover with water, add the onion and bay leaf then bring the liquid to the boil. Reduce the heat, cover and cook for 1–1½ hours, or until the chick peas are tender. Drain thoroughly, then remove the bay leaf.
Purée the peas and onion pieces. Mix in the lemon juice, garlic, oil, yogurt and cumin to make a fairly soft consistency. Add salt to taste.
Chill the hummus well, then garnish with parsley and black olives and accompany with the traditional pitta bread, warmed.
Serves 8–10

Hummus; Marinated mushrooms; Vegetable terrine

# Marinated mushrooms

| Metric | Imperial |
|---|---|
| 1 × 15 ml spoon cider vinegar | 1 tablespoon cider vinegar |
| 1 × 15 ml spoon olive oil | 1 tablespoon olive oil |
| 1 × 15 ml spoon lemon juice | 1 tablespoon lemon juice |
| few drops of Worcestershire sauce | few drops of Worcestershire sauce |
| 2 × 15 ml spoons tomato purée | 2 tablespoons tomato purée |
| 2 × 15 ml spoons cold water | 2 tablespoons cold water |
| 1 × 15 ml spoon chopped fresh mixed herbs | 1 tablespoon chopped fresh mixed herbs |
| 1 small onion, peeled and grated | 1 small onion, peeled and grated |
| 1 garlic clove, peeled and crushed | 1 garlic clove, peeled and crushed |
| 450 g button mushrooms, sliced | 1 lb button mushrooms, sliced |

Preparation time: 15 minutes

If using dried mixed herbs, only half the quantity will be required.

Place all the ingredients, except for the mushrooms, in a large screw-topped jar and shake well. Add the mushrooms, pushing them down if necessary. Shake the jar once again so the mushrooms are coated with the marinade. If you don't have a large screw-topped jar use any covered container.

Stand the jar in a cool place and leave for 24 hours, shaking occasionally so that the mushrooms soften. They will reduce in bulk considerably during this time and also produce quite an amount of liquid. Serve chilled with French bread.

# Vegetable terrine

| Metric | Imperial |
|---|---|
| 15 g butter | ½ oz butter |
| 4 tomatoes, thinly sliced | 4 tomatoes, thinly sliced |
| 350 g potatoes, peeled and coarsely grated | 12 oz potatoes, peeled and coarsely grated |
| 450 g spinach, cooked, well drained and chopped | 1 lb spinach, cooked, well drained and chopped |
| 100 g mushrooms, finely chopped | 4 oz mushrooms, finely chopped |
| 1 onion, peeled and grated | 1 onion, peeled and grated |
| 50 g Cheddar cheese, grated | 2 oz Cheddar cheese, grated |
| 2 × 15 ml spoons mixed fresh herbs, finely chopped | 2 tablespoons mixed fresh herbs, finely chopped |
| 2 eggs | 2 eggs |
| 2 × 15 ml spoons single cream | 2 tablespoons single cream |
| salt | salt |
| freshly ground black pepper | freshly ground black pepper |

Preparation time: 20 minutes
Cooking time: 1½ hours
Oven: 180°C, 350°F, Gas Mark 4

If fresh spinach is out of season, a large packet of frozen spinach can be used. Cook it as instructed on the packet, then drain and continue as in the recipe.

Grease the base and sides of a 900 ml/1½ pint soufflé dish with the butter and cover with the tomato slices keeping any leftover for later.

Mix together the potatoes, spinach, mushrooms, onion, cheese and herbs, then beat in the eggs and cream with plenty of salt and pepper. Turn the mixture into the prepared dish and arrange any remaining tomato slices on top. Cover with foil or a lid and cook in a preheated oven for 1½ hours. Leave to cool overnight then turn out and serve in wedges.

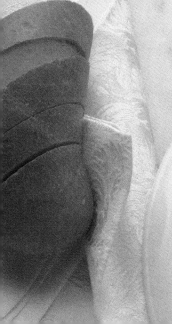

# SALADS

Always try to use the salad ingredients when absolutely fresh so that they still retain their distinctive flavour and texture. The other important part of a salad is the dressing, and many can be made in advance and stored in a screw-topped jar to use when required. Remember when dressing a lettuce-based salad to toss it at the last minute or the lettuce will go limp.

# Vinaigrette

| Metric | Imperial |
|---|---|
| 150 ml salad oil | ¼ pint salad oil |
| 3 × 15 ml spoons wine vinegar | 3 tablespoons wine vinegar |
| 1 × 5 ml spoon sugar | 1 teaspoon sugar |
| salt | salt |
| freshly ground black pepper | freshly ground black pepper |
| 1 × 5 ml spoon French mustard | 1 teaspoon French mustard |

Preparation time: 5 minutes

Put all the ingredients in a screw-topped jar, cover and shake well. Serve with salads. Any remaining dressing may be stored in the refrigerator.

# Four bean salad

| Metric | Imperial |
|---|---|
| 225 g French beans, halved | 8 oz French beans, halved |
| 450 g broad beans, shelled | 1 lb broad beans, shelled |
| 425 g can butter beans, drained and rinsed | 15 oz can butter beans, drained and rinsed |
| 425 g can cannellini beans, drained and rinsed | 15 oz can cannellini beans, drained and rinsed |
| 1 hard-boiled egg, finely chopped | 1 hard-boiled egg, finely chopped |

**Dressing:**

| Metric | Imperial |
|---|---|
| 6 × 15 ml spoons salad oil | 6 tablespoons salad oil |
| 2 × 15 ml spoons wine vinegar | 2 tablespoons wine vinegar |
| 1 × 15 ml spoon clear honey | 1 tablespoon clear honey |
| 1 × 15 ml spoon chopped fresh mint | 1 tablespoon chopped fresh mint |
| salt | salt |
| freshly ground black pepper | freshly ground black pepper |

Preparation time: 15 minutes
Cooking time: 5 minutes

Cook the French beans and broad beans together in boiling, salted water for 5 minutes. Drain, then mix with the butter beans and cannellini beans in a bowl. Put all the dressing ingredients in a screw-topped jar and shake well. Pour the dressing over the beans while they are still warm, then leave the salad to cool. Chill for 30 minutes. Scatter the chopped egg over the surface of the salad before serving with a savoury flan.
Serves 3–4

Vinaigrette; Four bean salad; Chinese salad

# Chinese salad

| Metric | Imperial |
|---|---|
| 275 g fresh bean sprouts | 10 oz fresh bean sprouts |
| 100 g button mushrooms, thinly sliced | 4 oz button mushrooms, thinly sliced |
| 1 bunch spring onions, chopped | 1 bunch spring onions, chopped |
| 1 chicken joint, cooked and shredded | 1 chicken joint, cooked and shredded |
| 1 banana, peeled and sliced | 1 banana, peeled and sliced |
| 1 × 200 g can peach slices, drained, chopped and juice reserved | 1 × 7 oz can peach slices, drained, chopped and juice reserved |
| 4 celery sticks, chopped | 4 celery sticks, chopped |
| 25 g cashew nuts | 1 oz cashew nuts |

**Dressing:**

| Metric | Imperial |
|---|---|
| 150 ml single cream | 1/4 pint single cream |
| 2 × 15 ml spoons soy sauce | 2 tablespoons soy sauce |
| 1 × 15 ml spoon malt vinegar | 1 tablespoon malt vinegar |
| 1 × 15 ml spoon reserved peach juice from the can | 1 tablespoon reserved peach juice from the can |
| salt | salt |
| freshly ground black pepper | freshly ground black pepper |
| celery leaves, to garnish | celery leaves, to garnish |

Preparation time: 30 minutes

Serve with ham or cold roast pork and fresh tomatoes, sliced and sprinkled with basil. Alternatively, slice the meat into thin shreds and stir into the salad.

Rinse and thoroughly dry the bean sprouts and put them into a bowl with the mushrooms. Add the spring onions, chicken pieces, banana, peach slices, celery and nuts.
Put all the dressing ingredients into a screw-topped jar and shake well. Pour the dressing over the salad and toss all the ingredients together. Garnish with the celery leaves.

# American mould

| Metric | Imperial |
|---|---|
| 1 lime-flavoured jelly | 1 lime-flavoured jelly |
| 150 ml dry cider | 1/4 pint dry cider |
| 2 celery sticks, chopped | 2 celery sticks, chopped |
| 1 green-skinned apple, quartered, cored and thinly sliced | 1 green-skinned apple, quartered, cored and thinly sliced |
| 1/4 cucumber, thinly sliced | 1/4 cucumber, thinly sliced |

| Filling: | Filling: |
|---|---|
| 225 g low fat soft cheese | 8 oz low fat soft cheese |
| 4 × 15 ml spoons milk | 4 tablespoons milk |
| 2–3 × 15 ml spoons chopped fresh chives | 2–3 tablespoons chopped fresh chives |
| 50 g walnuts, chopped | 2 oz walnuts, chopped |

Preparation time: 1 hour

Dissolve the jelly in 150 ml/1/4 pint boiling water. Stir in the cider with enough cold water or ice cubes to make the liquid up to 450 ml/3/4 pint. Pour a third of this jelly into a 1 litre/1 3/4 pint ring mould and scatter in the chopped celery. Chill until set.

Pour half the remaining jelly on top and arrange the apple slices around the ring. Chill again until set.

Pour in the remaining jelly, then place the cucumber on top of the apple, ensuring that all the slices are submerged in jelly. Chill the ring for 2 hours or until required.

For the filling, beat the cheese with the milk until evenly blended. Stir in the chives and walnuts.

To serve the mould, dip it in hot water for 20 seconds then invert it on to a plate. Fill the centre with the cream cheese mixture and garnish with a few extra chopped chives and walnuts.

Serves 4–6

# Rice salad

| Metric | Imperial |
|---|---|
| 225 g long grain rice | 8 oz long grain rice |
| 12 whole cardamom seeds | 12 whole cardamom seeds |
| salt | salt |
| 1 × 200 g can pineapple rings, drained and roughly chopped | 1 × 7 oz can pineapple rings, drained and roughly chopped |
| 1/2 cucumber, diced | 1/2 cucumber, diced |
| 50 g hazelnuts, roasted | 2 oz hazelnuts, roasted |

| Dressing: | Dressing: |
|---|---|
| grated rind and juice of 1 orange | grated rind and juice of 1 orange |
| 6 × 15 ml spoons salad oil | 6 tablespoons salad oil |
| 1 × 10 ml spoon curry paste | 1 dessert spoon curry paste |

Preparation time: 20 minutes
Cooking time: 15 minutes

This lightly curried salad goes well with cold chicken, pork and ham.

Cook the rice with the cardamom seeds in boiling, salted water for 10–15 minutes until the rice is just tender. Drain the rice and run cold water through the grains to remove any excess starch.

Mix the chopped pineapple into the rice with the cucumber and hazelnuts.

Put all the dressing ingredients in a screw-topped jar and shake well. Stir the dressing through the rice salad so that it is evenly coated.

# Fennel salad

| Metric | Imperial |
|---|---|
| 175 g–225 g courgettes, thinly sliced | 6–8 oz courgettes, thinly sliced |
| salt | salt |
| 1 large fennel, thinly sliced | 1 large fennel, thinly sliced |
| 1/4 cucumber, thinly sliced | 1/4 cucumber, thinly sliced |
| 225 g French beans, sliced and cooked | 8 oz French beans, sliced and cooked |
| 6 stuffed green olives | 6 stuffed green olives |

| Dressing: | Dressing: |
|---|---|
| 150 ml soured cream | 5 fl oz soured cream |
| 1 × 15 ml spoon mustard with seeds | 1 teaspoon mustard with seeds |

Preparation time: 30 minutes
Cooking time: 5 minutes

Put the courgette slices on a plate, sprinkle with salt and leave for 15 minutes to draw out the excess moisture.

Wash and thoroughly dry the courgette slices and place them in the bottom of a salad bowl. Place the thinly sliced fennel on top, then the cucumber and finally the beans.

Mix the soured cream with the mustard and pour it over the salad. Garnish with sliced olives, and chill for 30 minutes before serving.

Serves 4–6

American mould; Fennel salad; Rice salad

# Sweetcorn and pepper salad

**Metric**
1 × 300 g can sweetcorn
  niblets, drained
½ green pepper, chopped
½ red pepper, chopped
1 Spanish onion, peeled
  and cut into rings
1 bunch watercress

**Dressing:**
3 × 15 ml spoons salad
  oil
1 × 15 ml spoon wine
  vinegar
2 × 15 ml spoons chopped
  fresh parsley
pinch of sugar
salt
freshly ground black
  pepper

**Imperial**
1 × 11 oz can sweetcorn
  niblets, drained
½ green pepper, chopped
½ red pepper, chopped
1 Spanish onion, peeled
  and cut into rings
1 bunch watercress

**Dressing:**
3 tablespoons salad
  oil
1 tablespoon wine
  vinegar
2 tablespoons chopped
  fresh parsley
pinch of sugar
salt
freshly ground black
  pepper

Preparation time: 15 minutes

This salad is especially good with cold pork or ham.

Mix the sweetcorn with the green and red peppers.
Reserving the larger onion rings for garnish, mix the
rest into the sweetcorn mixture.
Put all the dressing ingredients in a screw-topped jar
and shake well. Toss the salad in the dressing.
Arrange the watercress around the outside of a salad
bowl. Spoon the sweetcorn mixture into the centre,
then garnish with the large onion rings.
Serves 4–6

# Tomato and avocado salad

**Metric**
4 × 15 ml spoons cooking
  oil
2 × 15 ml spoons vinegar
1 × 5 ml spoon dry
  mustard
1 × 5 ml spoon demerara
  sugar
1 × 10 ml spoon chopped
  fresh marjoram
salt
freshly ground black
  pepper

**Salad:**
4 tomatoes, peeled,
  quartered and seeded
1 avocado pear
100 g fresh dates, stoned
1 × 200 g can red kidney
  beans, drained and
  rinsed
few lettuce leaves

**Imperial**
4 tablespoons cooking
  oil
2 tablespoons vinegar
1 teaspoon dry
  mustard
1 teaspoon demerara
  sugar
1 dessert spoon chopped
  fresh marjoram
salt
freshly ground black
  pepper

**Salad:**
4 tomatoes, peeled,
  quartered and seeded
1 avocado pear
4 oz fresh dates, stoned
1 × 7 oz can red kidney
  beans, drained and
  rinsed
few lettuce leaves

Preparation time: 20 minutes (plus chilling)

Put all the dressing ingredients in a screw-topped jar
and shake well.
Put the tomatoes into a bowl. Halve, stone, peel, then
dice the pear and add it to the tomatoes with the dates.
Mix in the beans. Pour the dressing over the salad and
toss all the ingredients well together.
Line a dish with lettuce leaves, then turn the salad into
the centre and chill before serving.

# Salade nicoise

| Metric | Imperial |
|---|---|
| *few lettuce leaves* | *few lettuce leaves* |
| *1 × 200 g can tuna fish, drained* | *1 × 7 oz can tuna fish, drained* |
| *225 g French beans, chopped and cooked* | *8 oz French beans, chopped and cooked* |
| *225 g new potatoes, scraped, cooked and diced* | *8 oz new potatoes, scraped, cooked and diced* |
| *½ cucumber, sliced* | *½ cucumber, sliced* |
| *1 × 50 g can anchovy fillets, drained and halved* | *1 × 2 oz can anchovy fillets, drained and halved* |
| *little milk* | *little milk* |
| *black olives, halved and stoned* | *black olives, halved and stoned* |
| *225 g tomatoes, sliced* | *8 oz tomatoes, sliced* |

| *Dressing:* | *Dressing:* |
|---|---|
| *3 × 15 ml spoon olive oil* | *3 tablespoons olive oil* |
| *1 × 15 ml spoon wine vinegar* | *1 tablespoon wine vinegar* |
| *salt* | *salt* |
| *pinch of sugar* | *pinch of sugar* |
| *1 × 2.5 ml spoon French mustard* | *½ teaspoon French mustard* |
| *1 × 5 ml spoon finely chopped fresh mixed herbs* | *½ teaspoon finely chopped fresh mixed herbs* |

Preparation time: 30 minutes

Line a serving dish with lettuce. Place the tuna fish in the bottom and cover with the beans and potatoes. Arrange the cucumber slices on top. Soak the anchovy fillets in a little milk for a few minutes to remove some of the excess salt, then lattice them across the top of the cucumber with the olive halves in each diamond. Arrange the tomato slices around the edge.

Put all the dressing ingredients in a screw-topped jar and shake well. Pour the dressing over the salad at least 15 minutes before it is to be served so that the salad ingredients can absorb the flavour of the dressing. Serve well chilled with crusty bread.

Serves 6 as a starter or 4 as a main meal

Far left: Sweetcorn and pepper salad; Tomato and avocado salad
Left: Salade niçoise

# Coleslaw salad

**Metric**
1 × 15 ml spoon plain
  flour
1 × 15 ml spoon
  granulated sugar
salt
freshly ground black
  pepper
1 × 10 ml spoon French
  mustard
150 ml wine vinegar
15 g butter
1 egg
little milk

**Salad:**
350 g white cabbage,
  finely shredded
225 g carrots, peeled and
  grated
1 dessert apple, cored and
  chopped
25 g sultanas
25 g salted peanuts

**Imperial**
1 tablespoon plain
  flour
1 tablespoon granulated
  sugar
salt
freshly ground black
  pepper
1 dessert spoon French
  mustard
¼ pint wine vinegar
½ oz butter
1 egg
little milk

**Salad:**
12 oz white cabbage,
  finely shredded
8 oz carrots, peeled and
  grated
1 dessert apple, cored
  and chopped
1 oz sultanas
1 oz salted peanuts

Preparation time: 10 minutes
Cooking time: 10 minutes

Coleslaw is especially good with savoury flans. The dressing for this salad can be made several days in advance and kept undiluted in a cool place.

Put the flour, sugar, salt, pepper and mustard into a pan. Mix in a little vinegar to make a smooth paste, then gradually stir in the rest. Place the pan over a low heat and, stirring all the time, bring the mixture to the boil. Simmer for 5 minutes. Remove the pan from the heat and stir in the butter.
Beat the egg in a bowl, then gradually beat in the vinegar mixture. Return it to the pan and cook until it thickens. Leave to cool, then dilute with sufficient milk to make the required consistency. Taste and adjust the seasoning.
Mix the cabbage, carrots, apple, sultanas and peanuts together in a salad bowl, then stir in enough dressing to moisten the ingredients.
Serves 6

Coleslaw salad; Russian salad; Pasta salad

# Russian salad

**Metric**
450 g potatoes, peeled and
  cooked
100 g carrots, peeled,
  cooked and sliced into
  rings
100 g peas, cooked
2 celery sticks, chopped
2 gherkins, chopped
few capers

**Dressing:**
2 × 15 ml spoons salad
  oil
1 × 15 ml spoon wine
  vinegar
pinch of sugar
salt
freshly ground black
  pepper
150 ml mayonnaise

**Imperial**
1 lb potatoes, peeled and
  cooked
4 oz carrots, peeled,
  cooked and sliced into
  rings
4 oz peas, cooked
2 celery sticks, chopped
2 gherkins, chopped
few capers

**Dressing:**
2 tablespoons salad
  oil
1 tablespoon wine
  vinegar
pinch of sugar
salt
freshly ground black
  pepper
¼ pint mayonnaise

Preparation time: 20 minutes
Cooking time: 20 minutes

Serve this salad with any cold meats such as roast beef, pork or ham.

Cut the potatoes into small cubes and put them in a bowl. Add the carrots, peas, celery and gherkins.
Put the oil, vinegar, sugar, salt and pepper in a screw-topped jar and shake well. Toss the vegetables in the dressing and when they are well coated, then mix in the mayonnaise. Turn the salad into a serving bowl and sprinkle with the capers.
Serves 6

# Pasta salad

**Metric**
100 g pasta shells or twists
4 × 15 ml spoons salad
  oil
100 g peas, fresh or
  frozen
3 celery sticks, chopped
1 small bunch spring
  onions, chopped
6 black olives, stoned
  and chopped
25 g strip almonds,
  browned
100 g salami, sliced,
  skinned and chopped
1 × 15 ml spoon wine
  vinegar
salt
freshly ground black
  pepper
sprigs of watercress, to
  garnish

**Imperial**
4 oz pasta shells or twists
4 tablespoons salad
  oil
4 oz peas, fresh or
  frozen
3 celery sticks, chopped
1 small bunch spring
  onions, chopped
6 black olives, stoned
  and chopped
1 oz strip almonds,
  browned
4 oz salami, sliced,
  skinned and chopped
1 tablespoon wine
  vinegar
salt
freshly ground black
  pepper
sprigs of watercress, to
  garnish

Preparation time: 15 minutes
Cooking time: 10 minutes

Cook the pasta in boiling, salted water with 1 × 15 ml spoon/1 tablespoon of the oil for about 10 minutes, or until tender. Cook the peas with the pasta: if using fresh peas, they will take the same time, but frozen peas should be added half way through the cooking time. Drain well and run cold water through the pasta pieces to keep them separate. Leave to cool.
Put the celery into a bowl with the pasta and peas. Add the spring onions, olives, almonds and salami.
Mix the remaining oil with the vinegar and some salt and pepper. Pour it over the pasta salad and toss all the ingredients together.
Pile the salad into a serving bowl and garnish with watercress sprigs.

# Cauliflower salad

| Metric | Imperial |
|---|---|
| 1 cauliflower | 1 cauliflower |
| 3 streaky bacon rashers, rind removed | 3 streaky bacon rashers, rind removed |
| 100 g radish, trimmed and chopped | 4 oz radish, trimmed and chopped |
| 1 × 15 ml spoon capers | 1 tablespoon capers |

**Dressing:**

| Metric | Imperial |
|---|---|
| 4 × 15 ml spoons salad oil | 4 tablespoons salad oil |
| 4 × 15 ml spoons single cream | 4 tablespoons single cream |
| 2 × 15 ml spoons wine vinegar | 2 tablespoons wine vinegar |
| 1 garlic clove, peeled and crushed | 1 garlic clove, peeled and crushed |
| 2 × 15 ml spoons chopped fresh parsley | 2 tablespoons chopped fresh parsley |
| 1 × 5 ml spoon sugar | 1 teaspoon sugar |
| salt | salt |
| freshly ground black pepper | freshly ground black pepper |

Preparation time: 15 minutes
Cooking time: 3 minutes

This salad is particularly good served with cold chicken.

Cut the cauliflower into small florets. Wash and dry them thoroughly. Fry the bacon until crisp, then cut into small pieces and add to the cauliflower with the radishes and capers.

Put all the dressing ingredients into a screw-topped jar and shake well. Pour the dressing over the salad and toss the ingredients together.

**Variations:**

Replace the cauliflower florets with any one of the following ingredients:

225 g/8 oz fresh spinach, washed and shredded.
225 g/8 oz finely shredded Chinese lettuce.
450 g/1 lb fresh Brussels sprouts, trimmed and shredded.
450 g/1 lb calabrese flower heads, trimmed and washed.
450 g/1 lb courgettes, trimmed and thinly sliced.

# Watercress salad

| Metric | Imperial |
|---|---|
| 2 bunches watercress | 2 bunches watercress |
| few lettuce leaves | few lettuce leaves |
| 25 g walnut pieces | 1 oz walnut pieces |

**Dressing:**

| Metric | Imperial |
|---|---|
| 150 ml mayonnaise | 1/4 pint mayonnaise |
| 2 × 15 ml spoons wine vinegar | 2 tablespoons wine vinegar |
| 1 × 15 ml spoon salad oil | 1 tablespoon salad oil |
| 50 g Stilton cheese, grated | 2 oz Stilton cheese, grated |
| 1 × 5 ml spoon sugar | 1 teaspoon sugar |
| salt | salt |
| freshly ground black pepper | freshly ground black pepper |

Preparation time: 15 minutes

Thoroughly wash and dry the watercress and lettuce. Place the lettuce leaves around the edge of a serving dish with the watercress in the centre. Sprinkle over the walnut pieces.

Mix the mayonnaise with the vinegar and oil, then stir in the cheese and sugar and taste and adjust the seasoning.

Just before serving, spoon the dressing over the watercress and leave it for a few minutes.

Serves 3–4

# Red cabbage salad

| Metric | Imperial |
|---|---|
| 450 g red cabbage, finely shredded | 1 lb red cabbage, finely shredded |
| 225 g carrots, peeled and grated | 8 oz carrots, peeled and grated |
| 50 g raisins | 2 oz raisins |
| 2 large oranges | 2 large oranges |
| 4 × 15 ml spoons salad cream or mayonnaise | 4 tablespoons salad cream or mayonnaise |

Preparation time: 15 minutes

Put the shredded cabbage into a bowl with the carrots and raisins. Grate the rind from the oranges and mix it into the salad cream or mayonnaise. Using a sharp knife, remove all the peel and pith from the fruit. The easiest way to do this is to cut the top off the orange then cut spirally around the fruit just below the pith but above the flesh.

Cut the orange into segments between the membranes and add the pieces to the salad. Just before serving, mix in the orange-flavoured dressing.

Serves 4–6

# Potato salad

| Metric | Imperial |
|---|---|
| 450 g potatoes | 1 lb potatoes |
| 2 × 5 ml spoons salad oil | 2 teaspoons salad oil |
| 1 × 5 ml spoon vinegar | 1 teaspoon vinegar |
| 4 × 15 ml spoons soured cream | 4 tablespoons soured cream |
| salt | salt |
| freshly ground black pepper | freshly ground black pepper |
| chopped fresh parsley, to garnish | chopped fresh parsley, to garnish |

Preparation time: 10 minutes
Cooking time: 20 minutes

Potato salad can be made from either old or new potatoes. It is best to peel old potatoes first before cooking but for maximum flavour when using new potatoes cook them in their skins. They can then be peeled, although the skins give the salad a delicious nutty taste and texture.

Cook the potatoes in boiling, salted water for about 20 minutes until tender. Drain, and when cool enough to handle, cut the potatoes into 1 cm/½ inch cubes. Mix the oil and vinegar together and pour it over the potatoes while still warm so that they absorb the dressing. Leave to cool.
Using a wooden spoon, carefully combine the potatoes with the soured cream and plenty of salt and pepper, ensuring that you do not break up the pieces. Turn the salad into a bowl and sprinkle with parsley before serving.

**Variations:**
Substitute the soured cream with salad cream.
Stir 1 × 15 ml spoon/1 tablespoon creamed horseradish into the soured cream with 3 × 15 ml spoons/3 tablespoons chopped fennel.
Add 4 finely chopped spring onions to the salad with the soured cream.
While the potatoes are cooking, fry 50 g/2 oz finely chopped bacon in its own fat until crisp. After tossing the potatoes in oil and vinegar, mix in the bacon with any fat plus 50 g/2 oz finely chopped gherkins. Omit the soured cream dressing.
Stir in the oil and vinegar, then mix in 50/2 oz full fat soft cheese with garlic and herbs. Serve still warm as soon as the cheese has melted.

Cauliflower salad; Watercress salad;
Red cabbage salad; Potato salad

# MAIN MEALS

Although many of these dishes might be considered vegetarian, they make an interesting, delicious and often economical change for meat eaters also. One of the most important considerations when cooking main meals using vegetables is the seasoning, often the dish will require a little more than normal to bring out all the flavours.

# Cassoulet

| Metric | Imperial |
| --- | --- |
| 450 g haricot beans | 1 lb haricot beans |
| 2 × 15 ml spoons cooking oil | 2 tablespoons cooking oil |
| 450 g onions, peeled and sliced | 1 lb onions, peeled and sliced |
| 2 garlic cloves, peeled and chopped | 2 garlic cloves, peeled and chopped |
| 450 g carrots, peeled and sliced | 1 lb carrots, peeled and sliced |
| 225 g piece salt belly of pork or green cured bacon, rind removed, cut into small pieces | 8 oz piece salt belly of pork or green cured bacon, rind removed, cut into small pieces |
| 225 g spare rib of pork | 8 oz spare rib of pork |
| 1 breast of lamb, chopped | 1 breast of lamb, chopped |
| 3 × 15 ml spoons tomato purée | 3 tablespoons tomato purée |
| 1 large bouquet garni | 1 large bouquet garni |
| 100 g piece garlic sausage | 4 oz piece garlic sausage |
| salt | salt |
| freshly ground black pepper | freshly ground black pepper |
| 175 g–225 g fresh white breadcrumbs | 6–8 oz fresh white breadcrumbs |

Preparation time: 50 minutes
Cooking time: 4 hours
Oven: 150°C, 300°F, Gas Mark 2

Put the beans in a saucepan, cover generously with cold water, bring to the boil and simmer for 5 minutes. Remove the pan from the heat and leave the beans to soak for 40 minutes.

Heat the oil in a frying pan. Add the onions and garlic and cook for a few minutes to soften. Then add the carrots and fry until beginning to brown. Transfer to a plate.

Add the pieces of rind to the pan and cook until brown. Cut the spare rib of pork into cubes and brown them in the pan together with the pieces of breast of lamb. Stir in the tomato purée.

Drain the beans. Rinse them under cold water then return them to the saucepan with 900 ml/1½ pints of water. Slowly bring to the boil then pour into a 4.5 litre/8 pint casserole dish. Add all the other ingredients and season the mixture well with salt and pepper.

Sprinkle a thick layer of crumbs over the surface then cook the cassoulet for 3½–4 hours, pressing the crumbs down from time to time and adding more crumbs or more water if necessary. Complete the meal with a fresh, crisp salad.

Serves 8–10

Cassoulet; Stuffed peppers

# Stuffed peppers

| Metric | Imperial |
| --- | --- |
| 4 even size peppers | 4 even size peppers |

| Filling: | Filling: |
| --- | --- |
| 175 g streaky bacon, rind removed, chopped | 6 oz streaky bacon, rind removed, chopped |
| 1 onion, peeled and chopped | 1 onion, peeled and chopped |
| 100 g fresh white or brown breadcrumbs | 4 oz fresh white or brown breadcrumbs |
| 1 medium cooking apple, peeled and chopped | 1 medium cooking apple, peeled and chopped |
| 25 g walnuts, chopped | 1 oz walnuts, chopped |
| 1 × 5 ml spoon mixed dried herbs | 1 teaspoon mixed dried herbs |
| salt | salt |
| freshly ground black pepper | freshly ground black pepper |
| 1 egg, beaten | 1 egg, beaten |
| 1 × 15 ml spoon cooking oil | 1 tablespoon cooking oil |
| 2–3 × 15 ml spoons water | 2–3 tablespoons water |

Preparation time: 10 minutes
Cooking time: 45 minutes
Oven: 190°C, 375°F, Gas Mark 5

Cut off the stalk end of each pepper and carefully remove the core and all the seeds without breaking the sides. Stand the peppers in a deep dish. Cover with boiling water and leave for 5 minutes while preparing the filling.

Fry the bacon over a medium heat and as soon as the fat starts to run, add the onion and cook until softened. Remove the pan from the heat and stir in the breadcrumbs, apple, walnuts, herbs, salt and pepper. Mix in enough of the beaten egg to make a firm, moist mixture.

Drain the peppers well and stand them in a deep well-greased dish. Spoon in the filing, put on the 'hats' then brush with the oil. Add the water to the dish, cover with foil or a lid and cook in a preheated oven for about 35 minutes until tender. Serve with tomato sauce (see Stuffed Marrow Rings page 36), sauté potatoes and a braised vegetable.

**Variation:**

For cheesy peppers, substitute the bacon with 100 g/ 4 oz grated Double Gloucester cheese. Fry the onion gently in 15 g/½ oz butter or margarine, add the cheese with the remaining ingredients. Leave off the stalk ends: remove the foil for the last 10 minutes of cooking time and scatter the tops of the peppers with a little extra cheese and leave to brown.

# Vegetable fritters

**Preparation time: 30 minutes**
**Cooking time: 45 minutes**

| Metric | Imperial |
|---|---|
| 15 g lard | ½ oz lard |
| 1 small onion, peeled and finely chopped | 1 small onion, peeled and finely chopped |
| 15 g plain flour | ½ oz plain flour |
| 1 × 2.5 ml spoon dry mustard | ½ teaspoon dry mustard |
| 300 ml stock | ½ pint stock |
| 1 × 10 ml spoons malt vinegar | 1 dessertspoon malt vinegar |
| 1 × 15 ml spoon Worcestershire sauce | 1 tablespoon Worcestershire sauce |
| 1 × 15 ml spoon demerara sugar | 1 tablespoon demerara sugar |
| 2 × 15 ml spoons tomato purée | 2 tablespoons tomato purée |
| 1 × 15 ml spoon gherkins, chopped | 1 tablespoon gherkins, chopped |
| salt | salt |
| 175 g small whole carrots, scraped | 6 oz small whole carrots, scraped |
| 225 g cauliflower florets | 8 oz cauliflower florets |
| 175 g shallots or baby onions, peeled | 6 oz shallots or baby onions, peeled |
| salt | salt |
| 1 bay leaf | 1 bay leaf |
| 100 g button mushrooms, trimmed | 4 oz button mushrooms, trimmed |

**Batter:**

| Metric | Imperial |
|---|---|
| 100 g plain flour | 4 oz plain flour |
| pinch of salt | salt |
| 1 × 15 ml spoon grated Parmesan cheese | 1 tablespoon grated Parmesan cheese |
| 2 × 15 ml spoons sesame seeds (optional) | 2 tablespoons sesame seeds (optional) |
| 150 ml water | ¼ pint water |
| 1 egg white | 1 egg white |
| oil for deep frying | oil for deep frying |

To make the sauce, melt the lard in a saucepan, add the onion and cook gently until golden brown. Blend in the flour and mustard, then gradually add the stock, stirring well after each addition. Add the vinegar, Worcestershire sauce, demerara sugar, tomato purée, gherkins and salt. Bring to the boil, stirring, then cover and simmer for 10 minutes.

Meanwhile, cook the carrots, cauliflower and onions together in boiling, salted water for 5–7 minutes until just tender. Drain well.

To make the batter, sift the flour and salt into a bowl. Mix in the cheese and sesame seeds then gradually add the water, beating well until smooth and glossy. Whisk the egg white until it forms soft peaks and fold it into the flour mixture quickly and lightly.

Heat a deep pan half full of oil to 190°C/375°F. Dip the vegetables into the batter a few pieces at a time and fry them in the fat for about 10 minutes until golden brown. Drain on kitchen paper then serve with the barbecue sauce and complete the meal with a rice salad and watercress salad.

Vegetable fritters; Welsh leek pie; Vegetable loaf

# Welsh leek pie

| Metric | Imperial |
|---|---|
| 225 g plain flour | 8 oz plain flour |
| pinch of salt | pinch of salt |
| 50 g lard, cut up | 2 oz lard, cut up |
| 50 g butter or margarine, cut up | 2 oz butter or margarine cut up |
| 50 g butter | 2 oz butter |
| 750 g leeks, sliced | 1½ lb leeks, sliced |
| 100 g bacon rashers, chopped | 4 oz bacon rashers, chopped |
| 1 egg, beaten | 1 egg, beaten |
| 150 ml double or whipping cream | ¼ pint double or whipping cream |
| salt | salt |
| freshly ground black pepper | freshly ground black pepper |

Preparation time: 30 minutes
Cooking time: 40 minutes
Oven: 190°C, 375°F, Gas Mark 5

Sift the flour and salt together into a mixing bowl. Add the fats and rub them in until evenly distributed. Stir in sufficient cold water to make a fairly stiff dough and turn it on to a floured working surface. Knead gently until smooth then chill for 15 minutes.

Melt the butter or margarine in a saucepan, add the leeks, cover and cook over a low heat for 10 minutes. Stir in the bacon and leave the pan on one side.

Roll out half the pastry and line a 23 cm/9 inch deep pie plate. Turn the leek mixture into the centre and spread level. Mix the beaten egg and cream together, add plenty of salt and pepper and pour almost all of it into the dish over the leeks and bacon.

Cover the pie with the remaining pastry and decorate with pastry trimmings. Use the extra cream and egg mixture to glaze the pastry. Cook in a preheated oven until golden brown. Serve warm with creamed potatoes and baked tomatoes.

Serves 6

# Vegetable loaf

| Metric | Imperial |
|---|---|
| 100 g mushrooms | 4 oz mushrooms |
| 4 stuffed green olives, sliced | 4 stuffed green olives, sliced |
| 25 g butter or margarine | 1 oz margarine or butter |
| 1 large onion, peeled and chopped | 1 large onion, peeled and chopped |
| 100 g brown rice, cooked | 4 oz brown rice, cooked |
| 100 g peas, cooked | 4 oz peas, cooked |
| 1 × 15 ml spoon tomato purée | 1 tablespoon tomato purée |
| 1 × 15 ml spoon soy sauce | 1 tablespoon soy sauce |
| 1 × 2.5 ml spoon ground allspice | ½ teaspoon ground allspice |
| 2 eggs, beaten | 2 eggs, beaten |
| 2 hard-boiled eggs | 2 hard-boiled eggs |

Preparation time: 15 minutes
Cooking time: 45–50 minutes

Grease a 450 g/1 lb loaf tin. Line the base with a piece of greaseproof paper cut to fit and brush it with oil. Thinly slice two of the mushrooms and arrange them in a line down the centre of the tin and place a row of sliced stuffed olives on either side.

Melt the butter or margarine in a saucepan. Chop the rest of the mushrooms and add to the pan with the onions, then fry gently until beginning to soften. Stir in the rice, peas, tomato purée, soy sauce, allspice and beaten eggs. When the ingredients are thoroughly mixed, spoon half of the mixture into the base of the tin. Arrange the two hard-boiled eggs lengthwise in the tin and spoon the rest of the mixture on top, pressing it well down.

Put a piece of greased greaseproof paper on top of the mixture and cook in a preheated oven for 35–40 minutes or until firm to the touch. Leave to go cold in the tin then carefully turn it on to a serving plate and garnish with lettuce and tomatoes.

# Celeriac pancakes

**Preparation time:** 20 minutes
**Cooking time:** 55 minutes
**Oven:** 200°C, 400°F, Gas Mark 6

**Metric**
100 g plain flour
salt
1 egg
300 ml milk
a little oil

**Filling:**
25 g butter
750 g celeriac, peeled
 and cut into 1 cm
 pieces
225 g leeks, sliced
100 g peas, cooked
75 g cream cheese with
 garlic and herbs, cut
 up
2–3 × 15 ml spoons milk
celery salt
freshly ground black
 pepper
25 g cheese, grated
25 g flaked almonds
watercress, to garnish

**Imperial**
4 oz plain flour
salt
1 egg
½ pint milk
a little oil

**Filling:**
1 oz butter
1½ lb celeriac, peeled
 and cut into ½ inch
 pieces
8 oz leeks, sliced
4 oz peas, cooked
3 oz cream cheese with
 garlic and herbs, cut
 up
2–3 tablespoons milk
celery salt
freshly ground black
 pepper
1 oz cheese, grated
1 oz flaked almonds
watercress, to garnish

Sift the flour and salt together into a mixing bowl. Make a well in the centre and break in the egg. Gradually add the milk, mixing in the flour from around the sides as you work. When the batter is smooth, beat it well for a minute.

Heat an 18 cm/7 inch frying pan and grease it lightly with a little oil. When the pan is thoroughly hot, pour in enough batter to thinly coat the base. Cook over a medium heat until golden brown underneath then turn the pancake over and cook the other side. Make 7 more pancakes in the same way. Lightly greasing the pan after every third pancake. Keep the pancakes warm in a folded tea towel.

To make the filling, melt the butter in a large pan. Add the celeriac and leeks, cover and fry gently for 20–25 minutes until golden brown. Stir in the peas, cream cheese and a little milk to moisten, and add celery salt and pepper to taste.

Divide the filling between the pancakes and roll each one up. Arrange the pancakes in a shallow ovenproof dish. Sprinkle with the grated cheese and almonds and either brown under a preheated grill or place in a preheated oven for 15 minutes.

Serves 3–4

# Stuffed marrow

Preparation time: 25 minutes
Cooking time: 50 minutes
Oven: 200°C, 400°F, Gas Mark 6

**Metric**

15 g butter or margarine
1 small onion, peeled and
    chopped
2 rashers streaky bacon
15 g plain flour
1 × 425 g can peeled
    tomatoes
150 ml cold water
1 × 5 ml spoon horseradish
    sauce
pinch of nutmeg
bay leaf
salt
freshly ground black
    pepper
1 marrow, cut in half
    lengthways, seeds
    removed

**Stuffing:**

2 × 15 ml spoons oil
1 large onion, peeled and
    chopped
225 g cooked pork, minced
100 g fresh white bread-
    crumbs
1 garlic clove, peeled and
    crushed (optional)
1 × 5 ml spoon dried basil
grated rind and juice of
    ½ lemon
salt
freshly ground black
    pepper

**Imperial**

½ oz butter or margarine
1 small onion, peeled and
    chopped
2 rashers streaky bacon
½ oz plain flour
1 × 15 oz can peeled
    tomatoes
¼ pint cold water
1 teaspoon horseradish
    sauce
pinch of nutmeg
bay leaf
salt
freshly ground black
    pepper
1 marrow, cut in half
    lengthways, seeds
    removed

**Stuffing:**

2 tablespoons oil
1 large onion, peeled and
    chopped
8 oz cooked pork, minced
4 oz fresh white bread-
    crumbs
1 garlic clove, peeled and
    crushed (optional)
1 teaspoon dried basil
grated rind and juice of
    ½ lemon
salt
freshly ground black
    pepper

To make the sauce, melt the butter or margarine, add the onion and bacon and fry gently for 1 minute. Stir in the flour then, off the heat, blend in the tomatoes and their juice with the water. Stirring all the time, bring the sauce to the boil, then mix in the horseradish sauce, nutmeg, bay leaf, salt and pepper. Simmer, uncovered, for 15 minutes. Rub the sauce through a sieve or liquidize in a blender. Taste and adjust the seasoning.

Place the marrow in a pan of boiling salted water and cook gently for 5 minutes. Drain well and arrange in a greased ovenproof dish.

To make the stuffing, heat half the oil in a pan. Add the onion and fry gently until golden brown. Stir in the pork, breadcrumbs, garlic, basil, lemon rind and juice and plenty of salt and pepper. Bind the ingredients together with 4 × 15 ml spoons/4 tablespoons of the tomato sauce, then divide the filling between the marrow halves, packing it well down. Pour the remaining oil over the marrow halves and bake uncovered, for 20–25 minutes. Heat the remaining tomato sauce and serve separately.

Serves 6

Celeriac pancakes; Stuffed marrow

35

# Aubergine special

| Metric | Imperial |
|---|---|
| 1 aubergine (about 225 g), sliced | 1 aubergine (about 8 oz), sliced |
| salt | salt |
| 50 g butter | 2 oz butter |
| 50 g streaky bacon, rind removed, chopped | 2 oz streaky bacon, rind removed, chopped |
| 100 g shallots, peeled | 4 oz shallots, peeled |
| 100 g button mushrooms, trimmed | 4 oz button mushrooms, trimmed |
| 100 g tomatoes, peeled, seeded and sliced | 4 oz tomatoes, peeled, seeded and sliced |
| 8 stuffed green olives | 8 stuffed green olives |
| 150 ml red wine | 1/4 pint red wine |
| 1 × 15 ml spoon plain flour | 1 tablespoon plain flour |
| 150 ml double cream | 1/4 pint double cream |
| 25 g whole almonds, blanched | 1 oz whole almonds, blanched |
| freshly ground black pepper | freshly ground black pepper |

Preparation time: 25 minutes
Cooking time: 30 minutes

Place the aubergine slices on a large plate. Sprinkle salt over the cut surfaces, then leave the aubergine on one side for 10 minutes to draw out some of the excess moisture. Pat the slices dry with kitchen paper.

Melt the butter in a large pan, add the bacon and aubergine and cook them over a medium heat until beginning to soften. Add the shallots, mushrooms, tomatoes, 6 olives and the wine, then slowly bring to the boil. Cover and simmer for 15–20 minutes until almost tender.

In a small bowl blend the flour and cream together to a smooth consistency, then stir in a little of the hot liquid from the pan. Return the mixture to the pan, add the almonds and very slowly bring the sauce just to the boil. Taste and adjust the seasoning, then turn into a heated serving dish and garnish with the remaining olives, sliced. Serve with egg noodles and a selection of salads.

Serves 2

# Vegetable suet pudding

| Metric | Imperial |
|---|---|
| 350 g self-raising flour | 12 oz self-raising flour |
| pinch of salt | pinch of salt |
| 150 g shredded suet | 5 oz shredded suet |
| 1 large onion, peeled and grated | 1 large onion, peeled and grated |

| **Filing:** | **Filling:** |
|---|---|
| 350 g leeks, cut into 2.5 cm lengths | 12 oz leeks, cut into 1 inch lengths |
| 450 g carrots, peeled and sliced | 1 lb carrots, peeled and sliced |
| 450 g parsnips, peeled and sliced | 1 lb parsnips, peeled and sliced |
| salt | salt |
| 1 × 15 ml spoon plain flour | 1 tablespoon plain flour |
| grated rind and juice of 1 large orange | grated rind and juice of 1 large orange |
| 1 × 5 ml spoon dried sage | 1 teaspoon dried sage |
| salt | salt |
| freshly ground black pepper | freshly ground black pepper |
| 50 g butter | 2 oz butter |

Preparation time: 30 minutes
Cooking time: 3 hours

Sift the flour and salt together into a mixing bowl. Stir in the suet and grated onion with enough cold water to make a fairly soft dough. Grease a 1.75 litre/3 pint pudding basin. Roll out two-thirds of the dough and line the base and sides of the bowl extending the pastry just above the rim.

Place the leeks, carrots and parsnips into a saucepan. Add plenty of salt and cover with cold water. Bring to the boil, then immediately drain and run under cold water to cool quickly. Turn the vegetables into a mixing bowl. Stir in the flour, grated orange rind and juice, sage, salt and pepper. Pack half the vegetables into the lined basin. Place a knob of the butter on top, then add the rest of the vegetables and finish with the remaining butter.

Cover the pudding with the remaining dough, making sure the edges are well sealed. Make a pleat down the centre of a large piece of foil. Place it over the pudding and secure it with string. Steam the pudding for 2½–3 hours, replenishing the water in the steamer when necessary with more hot water. Serve with creamed potatoes and buttered cabbage or green beans.

Serves 6

# Cabbage hotpot

**Metric**
2 large chicken joints,
    skinned, boned and cut
    into bite-size pieces
2 × 15 ml spoons oil
225 g onions, peeled and
    sliced
450 g Dutch cabbage,
    shredded
2 × 15 ml spoons plain
    flour
2 × 15 ml spoons vinegar
300 ml chicken stock
2 × 15 ml spoons demerara
    sugar
salt
freshly ground black pepper
450 g potatoes, peeled and
    sliced
25 g butter, melted

**Imperial**
2 large chicken joints,
    skinned, boned and cut
    into bite-size pieces
2 tablespoons oil
8 oz onions, peeled and
    sliced
1 lb Dutch cabbage,
    shredded
2 tablespoons plain
    flour
2 tablespoons vinegar
½ pint chicken stock
2 tablespoons demerara
    sugar
salt
freshly ground black pepper
1 lb potatoes, peeled and
    sliced
1 oz butter, melted

Preparation time: 25 minutes
Cooking time: 1¾ hours
Oven: 180°C, 350°F, Gas Mark 4

Using a sharp knife, remove all the meat from the chicken joints. Simmer the bones and skin together for stock.

Heat the oil in a frying pan, add the meat and fry quickly until beginning to brown. Transfer to a plate. Fry the onions in the remaining fat until beginning to soften but not brown. Stir in the cabbage and cook together until all the fat has been absorbed. Mix in the flour, vinegar, stock, sugar, salt and pepper and bring to the boil. Stir in the meat, and turn the mixture into a 1¾ litre/3 pint casserole dish.

Cover with the sliced potatoes. Brush the surface completely with the melted butter then cook in a preheated oven for about 1½ hours until the potatoes are cooked and golden brown.

Aubergine special; Vegetable suet pudding; Cabbage hotpot

# Courgette and tomato gougère

**Metric**
350 g courgettes, sliced
2 × 15 ml spoons oil
25 g butter or margarine
2 medium onions, peeled
   and chopped
1 green pepper, cored,
   seeded and sliced
250 g tomatoes, peeled and
   quartered
1 × 5 ml spoon dried
   oregano
salt
freshly ground black pepper
2 × 5 ml spoons grated
   Parmesan cheese

**Choux paste:**
65 g plain flour
pinch of salt
50 g butter or margarine
150 ml water
2 eggs, beaten

**Imperial**
12 oz courgettes, sliced
2 tablespoons oil
1 oz butter or margarine
2 medium onions, peeled
   and chopped
1 green pepper, cored,
   seeded and sliced
8 oz tomatoes, peeled and
   quartered
1 teaspoon dried
   oregano
salt
freshly ground black pepper
2 teaspoons grated
   Parmesan cheese

**Choux paste:**
2½ oz plain flour
pinch of salt
2 oz butter or margarine
¼ pint of water
2 eggs, beaten

Preparation time: 30 minutes
Cooking time: 30–35 minutes
Oven: 200°C, 400°F, Gas Mark 6

Sprinkle the courgette slices with salt, then leave them on one side for 15 minutes to remove some of the excess moisture.

Heat the oil and butter or margarine together in a large frying pan, add the onions and cook slowly for 5 minutes. Stir in the sliced pepper. Rinse and drain the courgettes and add them to the pan. Cook for a further 5 minutes, stirring occasionally. Add the tomatoes, oregano, salt and pepper and cook for about 10 minutes until beginning to soften. Leave on one side.

Sift the flour and salt together on to a sheet of paper. Melt the butter or margarine in a saucepan, add the water and bring the liquid to the boil. When bubbling, draw the pan off the heat and immediately shoot in the flour. Beat the mixture until it is smooth and leaves the sides of the pan clean. Allow the paste to cool slightly. Gradually add the beaten eggs to the paste, beating well between each addition.

Spoon the mixture around the edge of a shallow 1.2 litre/2 pint ovenproof dish. Turn the vegetable mixture into the centre and sprinkle over the Parmesan cheese. Cook in a preheated oven for 30–35 minutes until the pastry is golden brown and well risen. Serve with a salad.
Serves 3–4

# Vegetable lasagne

**Metric**
50 g butter or margarine
225 g onions, peeled and
   sliced
1 small head celery,
   chopped
225 g mushrooms,
   quartered
1 × 750 g can tomatoes
1 bay leaf
1 × 5 ml spoon caster
   sugar
salt
freshly ground black
   pepper
100–150 g lasagne verde
300 ml plain unsweetened
   yogurt
75 g Cheddar cheese, grated
pinch of cayenne
1 × 2.5 ml spoon dry
   mustard
2 × 15 ml spoons rolled
   oats

**Imperial**
2 oz butter or margarine
8 oz onions, peeled and
   sliced
1 small head celery,
   chopped
8 oz mushrooms,
   quartered
1 × 1¾ lb can tomatoes
1 bay leaf
1 teaspoon caster
   sugar
salt
freshly ground black
   pepper
4–6 oz lasagne verde
½ pint plain unsweetened
   yogurt
3 oz Cheddar cheese, grated
pinch of cayenne
½ teaspoon dry
   mustard
2 tablespoons rolled
   oats

Preparation time: 15 minutes
Cooking time: 1 hour 25 minutes
Oven: 180°C, 350°F, Gas Mark 4

Melt the butter or margarine in a saucepan, add the onions and celery and cook for about 5 minutes until beginning to soften. Add the mushrooms and when they have absorbed all the fat, pour in the tomatoes and their juice and bring the mixture to the boil. Stir in the bay leaf, sugar, salt and pepper and boil rapidly, uncovered, for 20 minutes.

Pour half the vegetable mixture into the base of a 1.75/3 pint ovenproof dish, cover it completely with a layer of uncooked lasagne, then repeat the two layers once more, ending with a layer of lasagne.

Mix the yogurt with the cheese, cayenne, mustard, salt and pepper and spread it over the top of the lasagne. Sprinkle over the oats and cook in a preheated oven for 1 hour or until it is golden brown. Garnish with tomato slices. Serve with a salad or a hot green vegetable such as French beans.

# Stuffed cabbage leaves

| *Metric* | *Imperial* |
|---|---|
| 8 large cabbage leaves | 8 large cabbage leaves |
| salt | salt |
| 1 × 15 ml spoon cooking oil | 1 tablespoon cooking oil |
| 1 onion, peeled and coarsely chopped | 1 onion, peeled and coarsely chopped |
| 100 g long grain rice, cooked | 4 oz long grain rice, cooked |
| 50 g sultanas | 2 oz sultanas |
| 50 g salted peanuts | 2 oz salted peanuts |
| ½ × 5 ml spoon chilli powder | ½ teaspoon chilli powder |
| salt | salt |
| freshly ground black pepper | freshly ground black pepper |

| *Mushroom sauce:* | *Mushroom sauce:* |
|---|---|
| 15 g butter | ½ oz butter |
| 15 g plain flour | ½ oz plain flour |
| 300 ml milk | ½ pint milk |
| 50 g mushrooms, sliced and fried in butter | 2 oz mushrooms, sliced and fried in butter |
| salt | salt |
| freshly ground black pepper | freshly ground black pepper |

Preparation time: 20 minutes
Cooking time: 1 hour 20 minutes
Oven: 180°C, 350°F, Gas Mark 4

Chilli powder is very hot and varies in strength according to the manufacturer, so use it cautiously.

Blanch the cabbage leaves in boiling, salted water for 3 minutes. Drain thoroughly and leave to cool. Heat the oil in a frying pan, add the onions and fry gently until cooked. Stir in the rice, sultanas, peanuts, chilli powder and plenty of salt and pepper.
Place a spoonful of mixture on each cabbage leaf and roll the leaves into parcels, tucking the ends in well. Place the parcels close together in a lightly greased ovenproof dish, cover with foil or a lid and cook in a preheated oven for 30 minutes.
Meanwhile, melt the butter in a saucepan, stir in the flour and cook over a low heat for 1–2 minutes, stirring. Gradually blend in the milk and bring to the boil. Stir in the cooked mushrooms with salt and pepper to taste, then serve with the cabbage parcels.

Courgette and tomato gougère; Vegetable lasagne; Stuffed cabbage leaves

# Boston baked beans

Preparation time: 10 minutes
Cooking time: 4–4½ hours
Oven: 150°C, 300°F, Gas Mark 2

| Metric | Imperial |
|---|---|
| 450 g haricot beans, soaked overnight and drained | 1 lb haricot beans, soaked overnight and drained |
| 2 medium onions, peeled | 2 medium onions, peeled |
| 4 cloves | 4 cloves |
| 225 g pickled pork or green streaky bacon | 8 oz pickled pork or green streaky bacon |
| 3 × 15 ml spoons black treacle | 3 tablespoons black treacle |
| 75 g dark soft brown sugar | 3 oz dark soft brown sugar |
| 2 × 5 ml spoons made English mustard | 2 teaspoons made English mustard |
| 2 × 5 ml spoons salt | 2 teaspoons salt |

Place the beans in a large pan and cover with 1.2 litres/2 pints of water. Cover and simmer for 45 minutes until almost cooked. Drain, reserving 300 ml/½ pint of the bean water.

Spike the onions with the cloves and place them in the bottom of a 3½ litre/6 pint casserole dish. Score the rind of the meat and place it in the dish with the beans, treacle, sugar, mustard and salt. Cover and cook in a preheated oven for 3 hours, removing the lid for the last ½ hour if the mixture is still wet. Serve with fresh crusty bread and a green salad.
Serves 8

# Vegetable curry

Preparation time: 20 minutes
Cooking time: 1½ hours

| Metric | Imperial |
|---|---|
| 75 g butter or margarine | 3 oz butter or margarine |
| 450 g onions, peeled and sliced | 1 lb onions, peeled and sliced |
| 2 × 10 ml spoons curry powder | 2 dessertspoons curry powder |
| 1 × 5 ml spoon curry paste | 1 teaspoon curry paste |
| 1 × 5 ml spoon turmeric | 1 teaspoon turmeric |
| 1 × 2.5 ml spoon ground ginger | ½ teaspoon ground ginger |
| 1 × 1.25 ml spoon chilli powder | ¼ teaspoon chilli powder |
| 2 bay leaves | 2 bay leaves |
| 150 ml boiling water | ¼ pint boiling water |
| 2 × 15 ml spoons dessicated coconut | 2 tablespoons dessicated coconut |
| 225 g chick peas, soaked overnight and drained | 8 oz chick peas, soaked overnight and drained |
| 600 ml vegetable stock | 1 pint vegetable stock |
| 225 g tomatoes, peeled and chopped | 8 oz tomatoes, peeled and chopped |
| 25 g sultanas | 1 oz sultanas |
| 1 small cauliflower, divided into florets | 1 small cauliflower, divided into florets |
| 225 g carrots, peeled and sliced | 8 oz carrots, peeled and sliced |
| 1 medium leek, sliced | 1 medium leek, sliced |
| 1 dessert apple, cored and thickly sliced | 1 dessert apple, cored and thickly sliced |
| salt | salt |
| freshly ground black pepper | freshly ground black pepper |

Chilli powder varies in strength depending on the manufacturer, so it is best used cautiously.

Heat the butter or margarine in a large heavy saucepan or casserole dish, add the onions and fry gently until starting to brown. Stir in the curry powder, curry paste, turmeric, ground ginger, chilli powder and bay leaves and cook for a further 10 minutes, stirring occasionally.

Pour the boiling water over the coconut and leave it to infuse for 10 minutes then strain the liquid into the pan and discard the coconut. Add the drained chick peas, stock, tomatoes and sultanas and bring to the boil. Cover and simmer for 45 minutes.

Add the cauliflower florets, carrots, leek and apple to the curry. Bring back to the boil, then simmer for 20–30 minutes until all the vegetables are just tender. Taste and adjust the seasoning, then turn the curry into a heated serving dish. Serve with plain boiled rice, poppadoms and a lime pickle.
Serves 6

**Variation:**
Substitute 100 g/4 oz okra, trimmed, for the leek.

Boston baked beans; Vegetable curry; Vegetable pie with herb pastry

# Vegetable pie with herb pastry

Preparation time: 40 minutes
Cooking time: 1 hour
Oven: 190°C, 375°F, Gas Mark 5
 160°C, 325°F, Gas Mark 3

**Metric**
50 g butter or margarine
175 g onion, peeled and
 sliced
175 g carrot, peeled and
 chopped
225 g new potatoes,
 scrubbed and sliced
225 g broad beans shelled
225 g fresh peas, shelled
100 g mushrooms, sliced
225 g tomatoes, sliced
1 × 5 ml spoon yeast
 extract
just under 300 ml warm
 water

**Herb pastry:**
225 g plain flour
pinch of salt
50 g butter or margarine,
 cut up
2 × 5 ml spoons dried
 mixed herbs
milk to glaze

**Imperial**
2 oz butter or margarine
6 oz onion, peeled and
 sliced
6 oz carrot, peeled and
 chopped
8 oz new potatoes,
 scrubbed and sliced
8 oz broad beans, shelled
8 oz fresh peas, shelled
4 oz mushrooms, sliced
8 oz tomatoes, sliced
1 teaspoon yeast
 extract
just under ½ pint warm
 water

**Herb pastry:**
8 oz plain flour
pinch of salt
2 oz butter or margarine,
 cut up
2 teaspoons dried mixed
 herbs
milk to glaze

To make this pie in the winter when fresh peas and broad beans are not available, substitute half the quantity of fresh with frozen vegetables and do not thaw them out.

Melt the butter or margarine in a saucepan, add the onion, carrots, and new potatoes and gently fry for about 7 minutes, then turn into a large pie dish. Place the peas, beans and mushrooms on top, then arrange the slices of tomato on top of them. Leave the pie on one side.

To make the pastry, sift the flour and salt together into a mixing bowl, add the fats and rub them in until evenly distributed. Mix in the herbs then bind the ingredients together with enough cold water to make a soft but not sticky dough. Knead the dough lightly until smooth.

Dissolve the yeast extract in the water and pour in sufficient to come within 2.5 cm/1 inch of the rim of the dish. Roll out pastry and cover the pie, glaze the surface with milk, then leave the pie in a cool place for 15 minutes. Cook in a preheated oven for 30 minutes then reduce the heat and cook for a further 30 minutes until the pastry is golden brown.

Serves 3

# SUPPERS AND SNACKS

There is a large selection of supper and snack dishes based on vegetables. Baked and stuffed potatoes is one familiar idea, but many of these recipes would fit other occasions as well. Serve many of them with a salad and crusty bread to make a marvellous main course for lunch. Or follow a recipe, such as Smoked Fish Chowder, with a selection of cakes and you have created a delicious high tea.

# Pissaladière

**Metric**
175 g plain flour
1 × 2.5 ml spoon ground
   cinnamon (optional)
pinch of salt
40 g butter or margarine
40 g lard
1 egg yolk

**Filling:**
4 × 15 ml spoons oil
450 g onions, peeled and
   thinly sliced
2 garlic cloves, peeled
   and crushed
450 g tomatoes, peeled
   and chopped
1 × 5 ml spoon caster
   sugar
1 bouquet garni
2 × 15 ml spoons tomato
   purée
freshly ground black
   pepper
1 × 50 g can anchovy
   fillets
8 black olives

**Imperial**
6 oz plain flour
½ teaspoon ground
   cinnamon (optional)
pinch of salt
1½ oz butter or margarine
1½ oz lard
1 egg yolk

**Filling:**
4 tablespoons oil
1 lb onions, peeled and
   thinly sliced
2 garlic cloves, peeled
   and crushed
1 lb tomatoes, peeled
   and chopped
1 teaspoon caster
   sugar
1 bouquet garni
2 tablespoons tomato
   purée
freshly ground black
   pepper
1 × 2 oz can anchovy
   fillets
8 black olives

Preparation time: 25 minutes
Cooking time: 1 hour 15 minutes
Oven: 200°C, 400°F, Gas Mark 6

Sift the flour, cinnamon and salt together into a bowl. Add the fats and rub them in until the mixture resembles breadcrumbs. Mix in the egg yolk with a little cold water if necessary to make a fairly firm dough.

Knead the dough for a few seconds on a floured surface until smooth. Roll it out to a large circle and line a 20 cm/8 inch plain flan ring. Put in a cool place for 15 minutes.

Line the ring with greaseproof paper, fill with 'baking beans' and bake blind in a preheated oven for 15 minutes. Remove the paper and beans.

Meanwhile make the filling. Heat the oil in a frying pan, add the onions and garlic and fry gently for about 10 minutes. Stir in the tomatoes, sugar, bouquet garni, tomato purée, salt and pepper and bring the mixture to the boil. Reduce the heat and simmer, uncovered, for about 40 minutes. Remove the bouquet garni.

Spoon the tomato mixture into the flan case. Lattice the surface with anchovy fillets and place an olive in each diamond. Cook in the preheated oven for a further 20 minutes, brushing the anchovies and olives with a little extra oil if they become dry. Serve with a fresh green salad.

Serves 4–6

Pissaladière; Chicory rolls

# Chicory rolls

| Metric | Imperial |
|---|---|
| 4 medium heads chicory | 4 medium heads chicory |
| 4 slices (100 g) ham | 4 slices (4 oz) ham |
| salt | salt |
| | |
| **Sauce:** | **Sauce:** |
| 25 g butter or margarine | 1 oz butter or margarine |
| 25 g plain flour | 1 oz plain flour |
| 300 ml milk | 1/2 pint milk |
| grated rind and juice of 1/2 lemon | grated rind and juice of 1/2 lemon |
| 1 × 15 ml spoon chopped fresh parsley | 1 tablespoon chopped fresh parsley |
| freshly ground black pepper | freshly ground black pepper |
| 25 g Cheddar cheese, grated | 1 oz Cheddar cheese, grated |

Preparation time: 15 minutes
Cooking time: 20–25 minutes

Trim the base from each chicory head and remove any damaged leaves. Remove the hard core at the base of each head using the point of a knife. Cook the chicory heads in boiling, salted water for about 15 minutes until tender. Drain well.

Melt the butter or margarine in a saucepan. Stir in the flour, then gradually add the milk to make a smooth sauce. Add the lemon rind and juice and bring the sauce to the boil, stirring continuously. Cook for 1 minute, then add the parsley and salt and pepper.

Wrap a slice of ham around each chicory head and pack them close together in a 900 ml/1½ pint dish. Spoon the sauce over the top and sprinkle with cheese. Place under a preheated grill for about 10 minutes until golden brown. Serve with crusty bread.

# Courgette bake

| Metric | Imperial |
| --- | --- |
| 450 g courgettes, sliced | 1 lb courgettes, sliced |
| salt | salt |
| 1 × 15 ml spoon cooking oil | 1 tablespoon cooking oil |
| 25 g butter | 1 oz butter |
| 1 large onion, peeled and chopped | 1 large onion, peeled and chopped |
| 1 garlic clove, peeled and crushed | 1 garlic clove, peeled and crushed |
| 100 g sliced garlic sausage, chopped | 4 oz sliced garlic sausage, chopped |
| freshly ground black pepper | freshly ground black pepper |
| 50 g Cheddar cheese, grated | 2 oz Cheddar cheese, grated |
| 2 × 15 ml spoons Parmesan cheese | 2 tablespoons Parmesan cheese |

Preparation time: 10 minutes
Cooking time: 20 minutes
Oven: 190°C, 375°F, Gas Mark 5

This mixture, if baked in individual ovenproof dishes, makes a delicious first course. Reduce the cooking time by about 10 minutes.

Lay the courgette slices on a plate. Sprinkle liberally with salt and leave on one side to extract some of the excess moisture.
Heat the oil and butter together in a frying pan. Add the onion and fry gently until beginning to soften, then stir in the garlic and continue cooking until the onion begins to brown.
Rinse and drain the courgettes, then pat them dry. Add them to the frying pan and fry until lightly browned. Stir in the chopped garlic sausage, and salt and pepper to taste. Turn the mixture into a 1 litre/1¾ pint ovenproof dish.
Mix the two cheeses together, sprinkle them over the courgettes, then cook in a preheated oven for about 25 minutes until golden brown. Serve with crusty bread.

# Florentine eggs

| Metric | Imperial |
| --- | --- |
| 750 g spinach | 1½ lb spinach |
| salt | salt |
| 4 eggs (size 2) | 4 eggs (size 2) |
| 50 g butter or margarine | 2 oz butter or margarine |
| 50 g plain flour | 2 oz plain flour |
| 600 ml milk | 1 pint milk |
| 100 g Cheddar cheese, grated | 4 oz Cheddar cheese, grated |
| freshly ground black pepper | freshly ground black pepper |

Preparation time: 10 minutes
Cooking time: 10–15 minutes

Wash the spinach thoroughly and remove the thick, centre stem. Put the leaves into a large pan with no extra water. Add salt and cook, uncovered, for 10–15 minutes until tender and greatly reduced. Drain well. Meanwhile, melt the butter or margarine in a saucepan. Stir in the flour, then gradually blend in the milk to make a smooth consistency. Bring to the boil over a medium heat, stirring continuously and cook for 3–4 minutes. Mix in 75 g/3 oz of the cheese and add salt and pepper to taste.
Lower the eggs into boiling water and boil for just 3 minutes so they are still soft in the centre. Immediately plunge the eggs into cold water.
Chop the spinach, then stir a quarter of the sauce into it and divide the mixture between 4 individual dishes. Carefully peel the shells off the eggs and place one egg in the centre of each dish. Spoon over the rest of the sauce. Sprinkle the tops with the remaining cheese and put under a preheated grill for about 10 minutes. Serve at once.

# Vegetable risotto

**Preparation time: 20 minutes**
**Cooking time: 35 minutes**

**Metric**
1 small aubergine (about 225 g)
salt
2–3 × 15 ml spoons cooking oil
1 Spanish onion, peeled and sliced
225 g long grain rice
900 ml chicken stock
1 × 5 ml spoon dried marjoram
3 small courgettes (about 175 g), thickly sliced
1 red pepper, seeded and chopped
2 tomatoes, peeled and quartered
freshly ground black pepper

**Imperial**
1 small aubergine (about 8 oz)
salt
2–3 tablespoons cooking oil
1 Spanish onion, peeled and sliced
8 oz long grain rice
1½ pints chicken stock
1 teaspoon dried marjoram
3 small courgettes (about 6 oz), thickly sliced
1 red pepper, seeded and chopped
2 tomatoes, peeled and quartered
freshly ground black pepper

Trim off the ends from the aubergine, then cut it into 1 cm/½ inch cubes. Put them on a plate and sprinkle with 2 × 5 ml spoons/2 teaspoons salt. Leave on one side for 10 minutes to draw out the excess liquid, then rinse well.

Heat the oil in a frying pan, add the onion and cook over a low heat for 5–10 minutes or until beginning to soften. Add the rice and stir until it has turned opaque. Pour in 600 ml/1 pint of the stock. Bring to the boil, reduce the heat and simmer gently for about 15 minutes or until the liquid has been absorbed.

Meanwhile, simmer the aubergine and courgettes together in salted water for 4 minutes. Drain, then stir into the rice with the chopped pepper and tomatoes. Pour in the remaining stock. Continue to cook for about 5 minutes, stirring occasionally with a fork until the vegetables are tender and the rice moist but no longer wet.

Taste and adjust the seasoning. Complete the meal with hot, crusty bread.

Florentine eggs; Courgette bake; Vegetable risotto

# Stuffed baked potatoes

Potatoes baked in their skins are delicious served as an accompanying vegetable to the main course of the meal but they are equally nice baked, split, and then stuffed, for a supper dish. Allow 1 per person. To cook the potatoes, wash them well to remove any dirt, then prick the skin with a fork. Bake the potatoes on the open shelves of a preheated oven at 200°C, 400°F, Gas Mark 6, for 1–1½ hours, depending on their size. To reduce the cooking time slightly, bake the potatoes pierced through the centre with a metal skewer, which helps to conduct the heat. Alternatively, par-boil for 15 minutes, drain well then bake as usual. Cool slightly and either cut a large cross in the centre of the potato or cut the potato in half. Then scoop out the soft flesh inside, being careful not to damage the skin. Continue as in the individual recipe.

Preparation time: 10 minutes
Cooking time: 1–1½ hours
Oven: 200°C, 400°F, Gas Mark 6

# Tuna and onion filling

| Metric | Imperial |
|---|---|
| 2 potatoes, baked in their jackets | 2 potatoes, baked in their jackets |
| 1 × 75 g can tuna | 1 × 3 oz can tuna |
| 4 × 15 ml spoons mayonnaise | 4 tablespoons mayonnaise |
| 4 spring onions, trimmed and chopped | 4 spring onions, trimmed and chopped |
| grated rind of 1 small lemon | grated rind of 1 small lemon |
| salt | salt |
| freshly ground black pepper | freshly ground black pepper |

Cut the baked potatoes in half and scoop out the flesh into a bowl. Trim and chop the spring onions. Mix them into the potato flesh with the drained tuna fish, mayonnaise, grated lemon rind, and salt and pepper to taste. Pile the filling back into the potato shells and brown them under a preheated grill.
Serves 2–3

# Mushroom and cheese filling

| Metric | Imperial |
|---|---|
| 2 potatoes, baked in their jackets | 2 potatoes, baked in their jackets |
| 100 g button mushrooms, chopped | 4 oz button mushrooms, chopped |
| 25 g butter | 1 oz butter |
| 75 g Cheddar cheese, grated | 3 oz Cheddar cheese, grated |
| salt | salt |
| freshly ground black pepper | freshly ground black pepper |

Cut the baked potatoes in half and scoop the flesh into a bowl. Fry the mushrooms in the butter until tender. Mix in 50 g/2 oz of the cheese with plenty of salt and pepper and stir into the potato flesh. Return the filling to the shells, sprinkle over the rest of the cheese and brown under a preheated grill.
Serves 2–3

# Bacon and yogurt filling

| Metric | Imperial |
|---|---|
| 2 potatoes, baked in their jackets | 2 potatoes, baked in their jackets |
| 6 rashers (about 175 g) streaky bacon | 6 rashers (about 6 oz) streaky bacon |
| 3 × 15 ml spoons plain unsweetened yogurt | 3 tablespoons plain unsweetened yogurt |
| paprika | paprika |

Cut a deep cross in the centre of each baked potato and, using a tea towel to hold the potato, push in the sides to open out the cross. Cut the rind from the bacon. Roll up 2 rashers and skewer them with a cocktail stick. Grill all the bacon until brown and crisp. Chop the flat bacon rashers into pieces, stir them into the yogurt and spoon into the centre of the potato. Sprinkle with paprika pepper and garnish with the bacon rolls.
Serves 2

# Sausage and piccalilli filling

| Metric | Imperial |
|---|---|
| 2 potatoes, baked in their jackets | 2 potatoes, baked in their jackets |
| 2 sausages, cooked and sliced | 2 sausages, cooked and sliced |
| 2 × 15 ml spoons piccalilli | 2 tablespoons piccalilli |
| 25 g butter | 1 oz butter |
| salt | salt |
| freshly ground black pepper | freshly ground black pepper |
| chopped fresh parsley | chopped fresh parsley |

Cut the baked potatoes in half and scoop out the flesh into a bowl. Mix in the sausages, piccalilli, butter and plenty of salt and pepper. Pile the mixture back into the skins. Place under a preheated grill if necessary, then sprinkle over chopped parsley.
Serves 2

# Soured cream and chives filling

| Metric | Imperial |
|---|---|
| 2 potatoes, baked in their jackets | 2 potatoes, baked in their jackets |
| 2 × 15 ml spoons soured cream | 2 tablespoons soured cream |
| 1 × 15 ml spoon chopped fresh chives | 1 tablespoon chopped fresh chives |

Cut a deep cross in the centre of each baked potato, and holding the potato in a tea towel, push in the sides to open out the cross. Mix half the chives into the soured cream and spoon it into the cross, then sprinkle over the remaining chives.
Serves 2

Stuffed baked potatoes with (clockwise from top left): Tuna and onion filling; Mushroom and cheese filling; Bacon and yogurt filling; Sausage and piccalilli filling; Soured cream and chives filling

# Smoked fish chowder

| Metric | Imperial |
|---|---|
| 600 ml water | 1 pint water |
| 225 g smoked haddock | 8 oz smoked haddock |
| 2 streaky bacon rashers, rind removed, chopped | 2 streaky bacon rashers, rind removed, chopped |
| 225 g potatoes, peeled and cut into 1 cm cubes | 8 oz potatoes, peeled and cut into ½ inch cubes |
| 1 large onion, peeled and chopped | 1 large onion, peeled and chopped |
| 4 celery sticks, chopped | 4 celery sticks, chopped |
| 1 red pepper, cored, seeded and chopped | 1 red pepper, cored, seeded and chopped |
| 25 g butter or margarine | 1 oz butter or margarine |
| 300 ml milk | ½ pint milk |
| 2 × 15 ml spoons cornflour | 2 tablespoons cornflour |
| 1 × 200 g can sweetcorn kernels, drained | 1 × 7 oz can sweetcorn kernels, drained |
| freshly ground black pepper | freshly ground black pepper |

Preparation time: 15 minutes
Cooking time: 40 minutes

Chowder is a delicious fish soup that should be so thick with ingredients that it is almost a stew. If served with crusty bread, it makes a substantial supper dish.

In a large saucepan bring the water to the boil, add the fish and simmer for about 10 minutes until tender. Drain the fish, reserving the liquor, then flake the flesh discarding any skin and bones and leave on one side.
Fry the bacon in a large saucepan until crisp. Add the butter or margarine and when melted, stir in the potato, onion, celery and red pepper. Cook gently for 5 minutes until the onion and celery have softened. Make up the reserved fish liquor to 600 ml/1 pint with water. Simmer for 15 minutes.
In a small bowl, blend the cornflour to a paste with a little of the milk. Pour in some of the hot liquid and stir until smooth. Return this to the pan with the remaining milk and bring the soup to the boil, stirring. Add the flaked fish and sweetcorn and simmer for 5 minutes to heat them through. Taste and adjust the seasoning.
Serves 6

# Cabbage flan

| Metric | Imperial |
|---|---|
| 750 g cabbage (spring, summer, primo or Savoy) | 1½ lb cabbage (spring, summer, primo or Savoy) |
| 2 eggs (size 2), beaten | 2 eggs (size 2), beaten |
| 150 ml yogurt | ¼ pint yogurt |
| 150 ml single cream | ¼ pint single cream |
| 50 g Cheddar cheese, grated | 2 oz Cheddar cheese, grated |
| salt | salt |
| freshly ground black pepper | freshly ground black pepper |
| large pinch of grated nutmeg | large pinch of grated nutmeg |

Preparation time: 10 minutes
Cooking time: 35 minutes
Oven: 190°C, 375°F, Gas Mark 5

Remove the outside leaves of the cabbage and shred the heart finely. Place the large leaves into a pan of boiling, salted water with the shredded cabbage on top and cook for 5 minutes. Drain well, then separate the large leaves from the shredded cabbage and remove the thick parts of the stems.
Line the base and sides of a greased 20 cm/8 inch flan dish with 6–8 of the outside leaves, pressing them firmly into place.
Mix together the eggs, shredded cabbage, yogurt, cream and cheese with plenty of salt and pepper. Pour the filling into the lined dish and sprinkle the nutmeg over the surface. Cook in a preheated oven for 25–30 minutes or until the filling is set. The leaves around the edge may need to be brushed with a little oil during the cooking time so that they do not dry out.
Serves 4–6

Cabbage flan; smoked fish chowder

# Savoury triangles

**Metric**
1 × 225 g packet puff
  pastry, thawed
100 g full fat soft cheese
1 × 200 g can sweetcorn
  niblets, drained
4 spring onions, trimmed
  and chopped
salt
freshly ground black
  pepper
fat for deep-frying

**Imperial**
1 × 8 oz packet puff
  pastry, thawed
4 oz full fat soft cheese
1 × 7 oz can sweetcorn
  niblets, drained
4 spring onions, trimmed
  and chopped
salt
freshly ground black
  pepper
fat for deep-frying

Preparation time: 10 minutes
Cooking time: 20 minutes

Roll the pastry into a square a little larger than 30 cm/ 12 inches. Trim to size, then cut the pastry into four 15 cm/6 inch squares.

Beat the cheese until soft then mix in the sweetcorn, spring onions, salt and pepper. Divide the filling between the four squares, damp the edges and fold each square into a triangle, securely enclosing the filling.

Heat a deep pan half full with oil to 200°C/400°F and cook the rissoles one at a time in the hot fat. They will take about 5 minutes to turn golden brown. Drain thoroughly, then serve the triangles with peas.

# Spanish omelette

**Metric**
2 × 15 ml spoons olive
  oil
1 Spanish onion, peeled
  and chopped
1 large green pepper,
  cored, seeded and
  chopped
2 garlic cloves, peeled
  and chopped
2 tomatoes, skinned and
  chopped
4 eggs (size 2)
salt
freshly ground black
  pepper
1 × 15 ml chopped fresh
  parsley

**Imperial**
2 tablespoons olive
  oil
1 Spanish onion, peeled
  and chopped
1 large green pepper,
  cored, seeded and
  chopped
2 garlic cloves, peeled
  and chopped
2 tomatoes, skinned and
  chopped
4 eggs (size 2)
salt
freshly ground black
  pepper
1 tablespoon chopped
  fresh parsley

Preparation time: 10 minutes
Cooking time: 10 minutes

Heat the oil in a 20 cm/8 inch frying pan. Add the onion and fry gently until beginning to soften, then add the pepper, garlic and tomatoes and cook for 5 minutes, stirring.

Beat the eggs together, adding salt and pepper. Pour the beaten eggs into the pan and, with a fork, stir all the ingredients together until the eggs are beginning to set. Reduce the heat and cook the omelette until brown underneath. Place the pan under a preheated medium grill to set the top of the omelette. Sprinkle over the parsley and serve, cut into wedges, with a green salad.
Serves 2

**Variation:**
Cold cooked vegetables such as diced potatoes, beans and peas may also be added to the omelette.

# Carrot loaf

**Metric**
100 g plain flour
pinch of ground allspice
1 × 5 ml spoon bicarbonate
    of soda
1 × 2.5 ml spoon cream of
    tartar
pinch of salt
100 g wholewheat flour
225 g carrots, peeled and
    grated
100 g salted peanuts,
    chopped
1 × 15 ml spoon golden
    syrup
2 eggs
200 ml oil

**Imperial**
4 oz plain flour
pinch of ground allspice
1 teaspoon bicarbonate of
    soda
½ teaspoon cream of
    tartar
pinch of salt
4 oz wholewheat flour
8 oz carrots, peeled and
    grated
4 oz salted peanuts,
    chopped
1 tablespoon golden
    syrup
2 eggs
7 fl oz oil

Preparation time: 10 minutes
Cooking time: 1½ hours
Oven: 180°C, 350°F, Gas Mark 4

This rather unusual use of carrots makes a very delicious and moist loaf – perfect to serve with cheese for supper. It is best made at least a day before required, or it may be difficult to cut.

Grease a 1 kg/2 lb loaf tin and line the base. Sift the plain flour, allspice, bicarbonate of soda, cream of tartar and salt together into a mixing bowl. Stir in the wholewheat flour with the carrots and 75 g/3 oz of the chopped peanuts.
Beat the golden syrup, eggs and oil together and stir them into the dry ingredients to make a soft dropping consistency. Spoon the mixture into the prepared tin, then sprinkle over the remaining peanuts.
Cook in a preheated oven for 1½ hours or until the loaf is well risen and shrinking away from the sides of the tin. Cool the loaf in the tin for 10 minutes, then turn out on to a wire tray to cool completely. Store for 24 hours before use.
Serves 6

Savoury triangles; Spanish omelette; Carrot loaf

# Tomato and anchovy pizza

Preparation time: 25 minutes
Cooking time: 55 minutes
Oven: 220°C, 425°F, Gas Mark 7

**Metric**
175 g self-raising flour
salt
75 g butter or margarine,
    cut up
100 g cooked potato, sieved
    or well mashed

**Topping:**
1 × 15 ml spoon oil
350 g onions, peeled and
    chopped
350 g tomatoes, peeled
    and chopped
1 × 2.5 ml spoon oregano
1 × 15 ml spoon tomato
    purée
1 × 50 g can anchovy
    fillets
5 black olives, halved
    and stoned
100 g cheese, grated

**Imperial**
6 oz self-raising flour
salt
3 oz butter or margarine,
    cut up
4 oz cooked potato, sieved
    or well mashed

**Topping:**
1 tablespoon oil
12 oz onions, peeled and
    chopped
12 oz tomatoes, peeled
    and chopped
½ teaspoon oregano
1 tablespoon tomato
    purée
1 × 2 oz can anchovy
    fillets
5 black olives, halved
    and stoned
4 oz cheese, grated

Instead of the traditional yeasted bread base, this pizza has a delicious pastry base which is very quick and easy to make.

Sift the flour and salt together into a bowl. Add the butter or margarine and rub it in until the mixture resembles breadcrumbs. Stir in the potato and work the ingredients together until they form a soft dough. On a lightly floured surface, roll out the dough to a 20 cm/8 inch diameter circle and carefully transfer it to a large greased baking sheet.

To make the topping, heat the oil in a frying pan, add the onions and fry gently for about 5 minutes until softened. Stir in the tomatoes and oregano and cook rapidly for 10 minutes or until thick. Stir in salt and pepper with the tomato purée and spread the mixture over the pizza base to within 1 cm/½ inch of the edges. Sprinkle over the cheese, then arrange the anchovy fillets in a lattice design on top. Place a piece of black olive in each diamond. Cook in a preheated oven for 35–40 minutes until the base is cooked and the cheese golden brown.
Serves 4–6

From left: Tomato and anchovy pizza; Garlic sausage and sweetcorn pizza; Mushroom and pepper pizza

# Mushroom and pepper pizza

| Metric | Imperial |
|---|---|
| 1 quantity potato pastry (see Tomato and Anchovy Pizza) | 1 quantity potato pastry (see Tomato and Anchovy Pizza) |
| 2 × 25 ml spoons oil | 2 tablespoons oil |
| 225 g onions, peeled and sliced | 8 oz onions, peeled and sliced |
| 1 red pepper | 1 red pepper |
| 1 green pepper | 1 green pepper |
| 1 garlic clove, peeled and crushed | 1 garlic clove, peeled and crushed |
| 100 g mushrooms, sliced | 4 oz mushrooms, sliced |
| salt | salt |
| freshly ground black pepper | freshly ground black pepper |
| 100 g Cheddar cheese, grated | 4 oz Cheddar cheese, grated |

Preparation time: 25 minutes
Cooking time: 35–40 minutes
Oven: 220°C, 425°F, Gas Mark 7

On a lightly floured surface, roll out the pastry to a 20 cm/8 inch diameter circle and carefully transfer it to a large greased baking sheet.
Heat the oil in a frying pan, add the onions and fry gently until soft. Cut rings of pepper from each one, then core and seed the remainder and chop the flesh roughly. Add it to the onion with the garlic and mushrooms and cook for a further 5 minutes. Spread the mixture over the base. Cover with the cheese, garnish with the pepper rings and cook in a preheated oven for 35–40 minutes until the base is cooked.

# Garlic sausage and sweetcorn pizza

| Metric | Imperial |
|---|---|
| 1 quantity potato pastry (see Tomato and Anchovy Pizza) | 1 quantity potato pastry (see Tomato and Anchovy Pizza) |
| 1 × 200 g can sweetcorn niblets, drained | 1 × 7 oz can sweetcorn niblets, drained |
| 1 × 5 ml spoon cornflour | 1 teaspoon cornflour |
| 150 ml soured cream | 1/4 pint soured cream |
| 100 g garlic sausage, sliced | 4 oz garlic sausage, sliced |
| 2 tomatoes, sliced | 2 tomatoes, sliced |

Preparation time: 25 minutes
Cooking time: 35–40 minutes
Oven: 220°C, 425°F, Gas Mark 7

On a lightly floured surface, roll out the pastry to a 20 cm/8 inch diameter circle and carefully transfer it to a large greased baking sheet.
To make the topping, mix together the sweetcorn, cornflour and half the soured cream and spread it over the base. Arrange the slices of garlic sausage and tomato overlapping on top. Spoon over the rest of the soured cream and cook in a preheated oven for 35–40 minutes until the base is cooked.

# Danish cauliflower

| Metric | Imperial |
|---|---|
| 1 large cauliflower | 1 large cauliflower |
| 25 g butter or margarine | 1 oz butter or margarine |
| 25 g plain flour | 1 oz plain flour |
| 300 ml milk | 1/2 pint milk |
| 100 g Danish Blue cheese, grated | 4 oz Danish Blue cheese, grated |
| salt | salt |
| freshly ground black pepper | freshly ground black pepper |

Preparation time: 10 minutes
Cooking time: 25 minutes

Trim the cauliflower, leaving a few of the outside leaves in place, then make a deep cross into the base of the stalk. Cook the cauliflower in a pan of boiling, salted water for 15 minutes until cooked. Drain, then turn into a serving dish and keep warm.

Melt the butter or margarine in a pan. Stir in the flour, then gradually blend in the milk. Bring to the boil, stirring continuously, cook it for 3–4 minutes, then stir in 75 g/3 oz of the cheese with plenty of salt and pepper. Pour the sauce over the cauliflower and sprinkle the extra cheese on top before serving with freshly made toast. A tomato salad may also be served.

# Pan haggerty

| Metric | Imperial |
|---|---|
| 15 g lard or dripping | 1/2 oz lard or dripping |
| 450 g potatoes, peeled and thinly sliced | 1 lb potatoes, peeled and thinly sliced |
| 100 g cheese, grated | 4 oz cheese, grated |
| 225 g onions, peeled and thinly sliced | 8 oz onions, peeled and thinly sliced |
| salt | salt |
| freshly ground black pepper | freshly ground black pepper |

Preparation time: 10 minutes
Cooking time: 40 minutes

Melt the fat in a heavy-based frying pan about 20 cm/8 inches in diameter. Remove the pan from the heat, and arrange half the potatoes overlapping in the bottom of the pan. Sprinkle with salt and pepper, then cover with the cheese. Add a layer of onions, more salt and pepper, then make a final layer of potatoes.

Cover the pan and cook over a medium heat for 20 minutes or until the potatoes on the bottom are brown. Invert the mixture on to a plate then slip it back into the pan to brown the other side and complete the cooking. This will take about another 20 minutes. Serve the pan haggerty with a tomato salad.

# Wholewheat vegetable pasties

| Metric | Imperial |
|---|---|
| 100 g wholewheat flour | 4 oz wholewheat flour |
| 100 g plain flour | 4 oz plain flour |
| salt | salt |
| 50 g butter or margarine, cut up | 2 oz butter or margarine, cut up |
| 50 g lard, cut up | 2 oz lard, cut up |
| 2–3 × 15 ml spoons water | 2–3 tablespoons water |

| Filling: | Filling: |
|---|---|
| 100 g prepared broad beans | 4 oz prepared broad beans |
| 225 g turnip, peeled and diced | 8 oz turnip, peeled and diced |
| 225 g carrot, peeled and grated | 8 oz carrot, peeled and grated |
| 2 × 15 ml spoons chopped fresh chives | 2 tablespoons chopped fresh chives |
| 4 × 15 ml spoons mayonnaise | 4 tablespoons mayonnaise |
| freshly ground black pepper | freshly ground black pepper |
| beaten egg, to glaze | beaten egg, to glaze |

Preparation time: 15 minutes (plus chilling)
Cooking time: 35 minutes
Oven: 200°C, 400°C, Gas Mark 6

Mix the flours and a pinch of salt together in a bowl. Add the fats and rub them in until the mixture resembles breadcrumbs. Stir in sufficient water to make a fairly stiff dough. Turn the dough on to a floured surface and knead until smooth. Wrap in greaseproof and chill for 30 minutes.

To make the filling, cook the beans and turnips in boiling, salted water for 10 minutes or until just tender. Drain well, then stir in the carrot, chives, mayonnaise and salt and pepper. Leave on one side to cool.

On a floured surface, roll out the dough to 3 mm/1/8 inch thickness and cut out 4 × 16.5 mm/6½ inch circles, using a saucer as a guide. Divide the filling between the pastry rounds. Moisten the edges then lift them up over the filling to enclose it completely and form the shape of a Cornish pasty. Seal the edges and scallop them. Brush all over with the beaten egg.

Make a small air vent in the top of each pasty, then cook in a preheated oven for 25–30 minutes until golden brown. Serve warm or cold with a salad.

Pan haggerty; Danish cauliflower; Wholewheat vegetable pasties

# Egg and mushroom ramekins

| Metric | Imperial |
|---|---|
| 25 g butter | 1 oz butter |
| 100 g flat or button mushrooms | 4 oz flat or button mushrooms |
| pinch of grated nutmeg | pinch of grated nutmeg |
| freshly ground black pepper | freshly ground black pepper |
| 3 eggs (size 2) | 3 eggs (size 2) |
| 150 ml single cream | 1/4 pint single cream |
| salt | salt |
| 1 × 15 ml spoon grated Parmesan cheese | 1 tablespoon grated Parmesan cheese |

Preparation time: 5 minutes
Cooking time: 15–20 minutes
Oven: 180°C, 350°F, Gas Mark 4

Melt the butter in a small frying pan. Halve the mushrooms if too large and cook them in the butter for a few minutes until they start to brown. Add the nutmeg and pepper. Divide the mixture between 4 individual ramekin dishes.
Beat the eggs. Mix in the single cream and a little salt, then pour the mixture evenly into the dishes, making sure none of them are more than two thirds full. Sprinkle the Parmesan cheese over the top and cook in a preheated oven for 15–20 minutes until well risen and golden brown. Serve with crusty bread.

# Spaghetti with bacon

| Metric | Imperial |
|---|---|
| 175 g spaghetti | 6 oz spaghetti |
| 1 × 15 ml spoon cooking oil | 1 tablespoon cooking oil |
| 150 ml single cream | 1/4 pint single cream |
| 2 large garlic cloves, peeled and crushed | 2 large garlic cloves, peeled and crushed |
| 1 × 15 ml spoon chopped fresh parsley | 1 tablespoon chopped fresh parsley |
| 25 g pine kernels | 1 oz pine kernels |
| 100 g streaky bacon rashers | 4 oz streaky bacon rashers |

Preparation time: 5 minutes
Cooking time: 15 minutes

Pine kernels are available at health food shops. If, however, you find them difficult to obtain, substitute chopped walnuts.

Cook the spaghetti in boiling, salted water with the oil for 10 minutes until just cooked. Drain well and return to the pan.
Mix the cream with the garlic, parsley and pine kernels. Pour it over the spaghetti and stir all the ingredients together.
Fry or grill the bacon rashers until brown and crisp, then cut them into small pieces. Turn the spaghetti into a serving dish and scatter the bacon over the top. Serve with a mixed green salad.

# Cauliflower soufflé

**Metric**
1 medium cauliflower,
    broken into florets
40 g butter or margarine
40 g plain flour
450 ml milk
3 eggs (size 2),
    separated
75 g Cheddar cheese,
    grated
salt
freshly ground black
    pepper
pinch of grated nutmeg,
    optional

**Imperial**
1 medium cauliflower,
    broken into florets
1½ oz butter or margarine
1½ oz plain flour
¾ pint milk
3 eggs (size 2),
    separated
3 oz Cheddar cheese,
    grated
salt
freshly ground black
    pepper
pinch of grated nutmeg,
    optional

Preparation time: 10 minutes
Cooking time: 45 minutes
Oven: 200°C, 400°F, Gas Mark 6

Cook the florets in boiling, salted water for about 10 minutes or until tender. Drain well, mash almost to a purée then leave on one side.

Melt the butter or margarine in a saucepan. Stir in the flour, then gradually add the milk to make a smooth consistency. Bring the sauce to the boil, stirring continuously, and cook for 1 minute. Remove the pan from the heat and beat in the egg yolks, cheese and mashed cauliflower.

Whisk the egg whites until they stand in soft peaks. Then, using a metal spoon, lightly and quickly fold them into the mixture. Add salt and pepper to taste. Turn the cauliflower soufflé into a 1.5 litre/2½ pint soufflé dish and cook in a preheated oven for 30–35 minutes until well risen, golden brown and just set. Serve immediately with a green salad.

**Variations:**
For a spinach soufflé, substitute 450 g/1 lb spinach, cooked and finely chopped, for the mashed cauliflower.

For an onion and carrot soufflé, peel and roughly chop 350 g/12 oz onions and 225 g/8 oz carrots. Cook together in a little boiling, salted water for about 25 minutes until tender. Drain well, mash to a pulp, then mix in 1 × 15 ml spoon/1 tablespoon chopped fresh parsley. Stir into the soufflé mixture in place of the cauliflower.

Egg and mushroom ramekins; Spaghetti with bacon; Cauliflower soufflé

## ACCOMPANYING VEGETABLES

The vegetable dishes served with the main course of the meal can often determine whether the meal is a success or not. When choosing the vegetables, always bear in mind the combination of all the colours and textures once served on to a plate. Timing is important if you are to avoid overcooking. When served, vegetables should be only just tender and some such as carrots and French beans are nicest if left just a little crisp, although this is of course a matter of personal taste.

## Garlic beans

| Metric | Imperial |
|---|---|
| 450 g French beans, topped and tailed, cut into 6–7 cm lengths | 1 lb French beans, topped and tailed, cut into 2–3 inch lengths |
| salt | salt |
| 25 g butter | 1 oz butter |
| 2 garlic cloves, peeled and crushed | 2 garlic cloves, peeled and crushed |
| freshly ground black pepper | freshly ground black pepper |

Preparation time: 5 minutes
Cooking time: 10–15 minutes

Put the beans in a saucepan, add enough boiling water to cover, add some salt, then cover and cook for 10–15 minutes or until tender. Drain well.
Melt the butter in the pan in which the beans were cooked. Add the garlic and fry for 1 minute, then mix in the beans making sure they are well covered with the flavoured butter. Serve hot with a casserole such as coq au vin.

**Variation:**
Serve cold as a first course: cook the beans for 5–10 minutes until just tender. Toss in the garlic butter and leave to cool. Serve sprinkled with paprika and sieved hard-boiled egg.

Garlic beans; Creamed swede and carrot

# Creamed swede and carrot

**Metric**
750 g swedes, peeled and
  diced
225 g carrots, peeled and
  sliced
salt
25 g butter
2 × 15 ml spoons milk
1 × 200 g can sweetcorn
  niblets, drained
freshly ground black
  pepper
3 large tomatoes, sliced
25 g fresh white bread-
  crumbs

**Imperial**
1½ lb swedes, peeled and
  diced
8 oz carrots, peeled and
  sliced
salt
1 oz butter
2 tablespoons milk
1 × 7 oz can sweetcorn
  niblets, drained
freshly ground black
  pepper
3 large tomatoes, sliced
1 oz fresh white bread-
  crumbs

Preparation time: 10 minutes
Cooking time: 40 minutes

This dish can be made up in advance, left to cool, then
placed in a preheated oven at 180°C, 350°F, Gas Mark
4 for 30 minutes.

Cook the swede and carrots together in boiling, salted
water for about 10 minutes until just tender. Drain
them well, then roughly mash together. Beat in half
the butter with the milk, sweetcorn, salt and pepper.
Turn the mixture into a 1.2 litre/2 pint casserole dish.
Arrange the sliced tomatoes on top, sprinkle over the
breadcrumbs, then dot the surface with the remaining
butter. Put under a preheated hot grill until the top is
crisp and brown.

# Spring carrots

Preparation time: 10 minutes
Cooking time: 20 minutes

| Metric | Imperial |
|---|---|
| 25 g butter | 1 oz butter |
| 1 × 15 ml spoon oil | 1 tablespoon oil |
| 1 medium onion, peeled and finely chopped | 1 medium onion, peeled and finely chopped |
| 750 g carrots, peeled and sliced | 1½ lb carrots, peeled and sliced |
| 1 × 15 ml spoon demerara sugar | 1 tablespoon demerara sugar |
| 1 × 15 ml spoon water | 1 tablespoon water |
| salt | salt |
| freshly ground black pepper | freshly ground black pepper |
| 1 × 5 ml spoon chopped fresh thyme | 1 teaspoon chopped fresh thyme |

Put the butter and oil into a large pan. Add the onion, carrots, sugar, water, salt and pepper. Cover and cook over a low heat for about 15 minutes, stirring occasionally until the carrots are just tender.

Remove the lid for the last 5 minutes of cooking time and, if there is a lot of liquid, boil it rapidly until reduced and the carrots are glazed. Turn the vegetables into a warm serving dish, sprinkle with the chopped thyme and serve with a roast meat such as beef or lamb.

# Oven-baked spinach with turnips

Preparation time: 15 minutes
Cooking time: 45 minutes
Oven: 160°C, 325°F, Gas Mark 3

| Metric | Imperial |
|---|---|
| 450 g spinach | 1 lb spinach |
| salt | salt |
| 225 g turnip, peeled and coarsely grated | 8 oz turnip, peeled and coarsely grated |
| 2 eggs | 2 eggs |
| 300 ml milk | ½ pint milk |
| 1 × 1.25 ml spoon grated nutmeg | ¼ teaspoon grated nutmeg |
| freshly ground black pepper | freshly ground black pepper |
| 15–25 g Parmesan cheese, grated | ½–1 oz Parmesan cheese, grated |

Rinse a large pan out with water. Add the spinach straight from the final rinse water, sprinkle over some salt, then cover and cook for about 5 minutes until tender. Drain very thoroughly, then chop.

Lightly beat the eggs together, add the milk, nutmeg, salt and pepper. Stir in the grated turnip and chopped spinach. Pour the mixture into a lightly greased 900 ml/1½ pint dish and bake in a preheated oven for 45 minutes until the custard is set and the top is brown.

# Garlic swedes

Preparation time: 10 minutes
Cooking time: 25 minutes

| Metric | Imperial |
|---|---|
| 750 g swedes, peeled and diced | 1½ lb swedes, peeled and diced |
| salt | salt |
| 1 sprig rosemary | 1 sprig rosemary |
| 50 g butter | 2 oz butter |
| 1 garlic clove, peeled and crushed | 1 garlic clove, peeled and crushed |
| 75 g fresh white breadcrumbs | 3 oz fresh white breadcrumbs |
| 2 × 15 ml spoons mayonnaise | 2 tablespoons mayonnaise |

Cook the swedes in boiling, salted water with the sprig of rosemary for 15 minutes until tender.

Meanwhile, melt the butter, add the garlic and fry for 1 minute. Stir in the breadcrumbs and cook over a fairly high heat until golden brown.

Drain the swedes, remove the rosemary sprig, then mix in the mayonnaise. When the pieces of swede are thoroughly coated, turn them into a serving dish and sprinkle over the breadcrumbs mixture. Serve with roast beef.

# Celeriac with mustard sauce

**Preparation time:** 15 minutes
**Cooking time:** 35 minutes
**Oven:** 190°C, 375°F, Gas Mark 5

**Metric**
750 g celeriac, peeled and cut into 1 cm pieces

**Sauce:**
25 g butter or margarine
1 small onion, peeled and finely chopped
15 g plain flour
1 × 5 ml spoon dry mustard
1 × 15 ml spoon vinegar
1 × 5 ml spoon sugar
150 ml milk and vegetable cooking water, mixed
salt
freshly ground black pepper
2 × 15 ml spoons fresh breadcrumbs
25 g cheese, grated

**Imperial**
1½ lb celeriac, peeled and cut into ½ inch pieces

**Sauce:**
1 oz butter or margarine
1 small onion, peeled and finely chopped
½ oz plain flour
1 teaspoon dry mustard
1 tablespoon vinegar
1 teaspoon sugar
¼ pint milk and vegetable cooking water, mixed
salt
freshly ground black pepper
2 tablespoons fresh breadcrumbs
1 oz cheese, grated

Cook the celeriac pieces in boiling, salted water for 10–15 minutes until just tender. Drain, reserving some of the cooking water for the sauce.

Heat the butter or margarine in a pan, add the onion and fry over a low heat until tender and just starting to brown. Stir in the flour and mustard powder. Remove the pan from the heat and add the vinegar, sugar and gradually blend in the milk and reserved cooking water mixed. Bring to the boil, stirring, then simmer for 3 minutes. Add salt and pepper to taste.

Stir the cooked celeriac into the sauce and spoon the mixture into a 600–750 ml/1–1½ pint ovenproof dish. Mix together the breadcrumbs and cheese and sprinkle over the top. Brown under a preheated grill or place in a preheated oven for 15 minutes.

Spring carrots; Garlic swedes; Celeriac with mustard sauce; Oven-baked spinach with turnips

# Pommes duchesse

| Metric | Imperial |
|---|---|
| 750 g potatoes, peeled | 1½ lb potatoes, peeled |
| 25 g butter (optional) | 1 oz butter (optional) |
| 1 egg (size 2), beaten | 1 egg (size 2), beaten |
| salt | salt |
| freshly ground black pepper | freshly ground black pepper |
| grated nutmeg | grated nutmeg |

Preparation time: 15 minutes
Cooking time: 45 minutes
Oven: 190°C, 375°F, Gas Mark 5

This recipe freezes very well. Pipe the potato on to a greased baking sheet and open freeze for 24 hours, then transfer to rigid containers and keep for up to 3 months. Brush with the egg glaze while still frozen, then thaw and continue as in the recipe.

Cook the potatoes in boiling, salted water for about 25 minutes until tender. Drain, then mash until smooth. Stir in the butter and 1 × 10 ml spoon/1 dessertspoon of the beaten egg with salt, pepper and nutmeg to taste. Pipe the mixture on to greased baking sheets in large rosettes. Leave to cool.
Carefully brush the surface with beaten egg, then either bake for about 15 minutes in a preheated oven or brown under a preheated hot grill.

# Pommes boulangère

| Metric | Imperial |
|---|---|
| 50 g butter | 2 oz butter |
| 1 kg potatoes, peeled and sliced | 2 lb potatoes, peeled and sliced |
| 2 medium onions, peeled and sliced | 2 medium onions, peeled and sliced |
| salt | salt |
| freshly ground black pepper | freshly ground black pepper |
| 300 ml chicken stock | ½ pint chicken stock |

Preparation time: 15 minutes
Cooking time: 1½–2 hours
Oven: 160°C, 325°F, Gas Mark 3

Grease a 1.2 litre/2 pint ovenproof dish with 25 g/1 oz of the butter. Arrange the potatoes and onions in alternate layers, adding plenty of salt and pepper between each layer, ending with a neat layer of potato slices on top.
Pour over the stock then dot the surface with the rest of the butter. Cover the dish with the lid or foil and bake in a preheated oven for 1½–2 hours, removing the cover after 1 hour to allow the top layer of potatoes to brown.

# Pommes sautées

| Metric | Imperial |
|---|---|
| 50 g butter | 2 oz butter |
| 2 × 15 ml spoons oil | 2 tablespoons oil |
| 750 g cooked potatoes, fairly thickly sliced | 1½ lb cooked potatoes, fairly thickly sliced |
| salt | salt |
| chopped fresh parsley | chopped fresh parsley |

Preparation time: 10 minutes
Cooking time: 10 minutes

Heat the butter and oil together in a large frying pan. Add the potatoes and fry gently for about 10 minutes, turning them often until golden brown on both sides. Sprinkle with salt and parsley just before serving.

**Variation:**
For pommes à la lyonnaise, prepare as above and, when almost cooked, add 1 large onion, peeled, sliced and fried in butter. Finish by cooking together, stirring or shaking the pan frequently so that the two vegetables mix. Serve sprinkled with parsley.

Pommes duchesse; Pommes boulangère; Pommes sautées

# Hot red cabbage

| Metric | Imperial |
|---|---|
| 1 kg red cabbage, shredded | 2 lb red cabbage, shredded |
| 50 g butter | 2 oz butter |
| 1 × 15 ml spoon cooking oil | 1 tablespoon cooking oil |
| 1 large onion, peeled and sliced | 1 large onion, peeled and sliced |
| 1 garlic clove, peeled and crushed | 1 garlic clove, peeled and crushed |
| 225 g cooking apple, peeled, cored and thickly sliced | 8 oz cooking apple, peeled, cored and thickly sliced |
| 1 × 1.25 ml spoon grated nutmeg | 1/4 teaspoon grated nutmeg |
| 1 × 2.5 ml spoon caraway seeds | 1/2 teaspoon caraway seeds |
| 3 × 15 ml spoons demerara sugar | 3 tablespoons demerara sugar |
| 4 × 15 ml spoons water | 4 tablespoons water |
| 4 × 15 ml spoons wine vinegar | 4 tablespoons wine vinegar |
| salt | salt |
| freshly ground black pepper | freshly ground black pepper |

Preparation time: 10 minutes
Cooking time: 1 hour

Melt the butter and oil in a large saucepan, add the onion and garlic and fry for about 5 minutes until beginning to soften. Stir in the apple, nutmeg, caraway seeds, sugar and cabbage. Pour in the water and vinegar.
Cover and simmer for about 45 minutes or until tender, stirring occasionally. Add salt and pepper to taste then turn into a serving dish. This is especially good with pork dishes.
Serves 4–6

# Braised cabbage

| Metric | Imperial |
|---|---|
| 25 g lard | 1 oz lard |
| 225 g onions, peeled and sliced | 8 oz onions, peeled and sliced |
| 750 g white Dutch cabbage, shredded | 1 1/2 lb white Dutch cabbage, shredded |
| salt | salt |
| freshly ground black pepper | freshly ground black pepper |
| 1 × 2.5 ml spoon grated nutmeg | 1/2 teaspoon grated nutmeg |
| 25 g raisins | 1 oz raisins |
| 25 g salted peanuts | 1 oz salted peanuts |

Preparation time: 10 minutes
Cooking time: 45 minutes

Melt the lard in a large saucepan. Add the onion and cook for a few minutes until beginning to soften. Stir in the cabbage, salt, pepper and nutmeg. Cover and cook over a low heat for 20 minutes, stirring.
Add the raisins, cover and cook for a further 20 minutes or until all the vegetables are tender.
Turn the mixture into a warm serving dish, sprinkle over the peanuts and serve with pork or chicken-based dishes.
Serves 4–6

Cabbage with ham and cream;
Braised cabbage; Hot red cabbage

# Cabbage with ham and cream

| Metric | Imperial |
|---|---|
| 750 g cabbage or greens | 1 1/2 lb cabbage or greens |
| 25 g butter | 1 oz butter |
| 1 × 15 ml spoon oil | 1 tablespoon oil |
| 1 medium onion, peeled and sliced | 1 medium onion, peeled and sliced |
| salt | salt |
| 1 × 5 ml spoon paprika | 1 teaspoon paprika |
| 100 g ham, chopped | 4 oz ham, chopped |
| 150 ml soured cream | 1/4 pint soured cream |

Preparation time: 5 minutes
Cooking time: 50 minutes
Oven: 180°C, 350°F, Gas Mark 4

Remove the thick stems from the cabbage or greens, then shred the leaves into 1 cm/1/2 inch strips.
Heat the butter and oil together in a large saucepan, add the onion and cabbage and cook, stirring occasionally, for about 10 minutes or until the fat is almost absorbed. Stir in the salt, paprika, ham and almost all the soured cream. Turn the mixture into a 1 litre/1 3/4 pint casserole dish, cover and cook for 40 minutes at 180°C, 350°F, Gas Mark 4 until tender.
Stir the ingredients well before serving with the remainder of the soured cream spooned over.

# Brussels sprouts with chestnuts

| Metric | Imperial |
|---|---|
| *1 kg Brussels sprouts* | *2 lb Brussels sprouts* |
| *225 g chestnuts* | *8 oz chestnuts* |
| *salt* | *salt* |
| *25 g butter* | *1 oz butter* |
| *grated rind and juice of* | *grated rind and juice of* |
| *½ lemon* | *½ lemon* |

Preparation time: 15 minutes
Cooking time: 20 minutes

Trim the Brussels sprouts, removing any damaged outer leaves and cut a small cross in the base of each stalk.
Snip the tops of the chestnuts with a pair of scissors. Put them into a saucepan, cover with cold water and bring to the boil. Boil for 3 minutes, then remove the chestnuts one at a time. Allow to cool a little and peel off both the outer and inner skins.
Cook the Brussels sprouts in boiling, salted water for 15 minutes, adding the peeled chestnuts for the last 5 minutes of cooking time. Drain well. Melt the butter in the same pan. Add the lemon rind and juice, return the Brussels sprouts and chestnuts to the pan and toss them well in the butter before serving. This dish is especially good served with roast turkey.
Serves 6

**Variation:**
Omit lemon rind and juice and stir 75 g/3 oz chopped cooked streaky bacon into the cooked Brussels sprouts with 150 ml/¼ pint soured cream. The chestnuts may be omitted, in which case it would serve 4–6 people.

# Beetroot with orange and horseradish sauce

| Metric | Imperial |
|---|---|
| *450 g raw beetroot* | *1 lb raw beetroot* |
| *salt* | *salt* |
| *1 × 15 ml spoon chopped* | *1 tablespoon chopped* |
| *fresh parsley* | *fresh parsley* |
| | |
| ***Sauce:*** | ***Sauce:*** |
| *25 g butter or margarine* | *1 oz butter or margarine* |
| *25 g plain flour* | *1 oz plain flour* |
| *300 ml milk* | *½ pint milk* |
| *freshly ground black* | *freshly ground black* |
| *pepper* | *pepper* |
| *grated rind and juice of* | *grated rind and juice of* |
| *1 orange* | *1 orange* |
| *2 × 15 ml spoons cream of* | *2 tablespoons cream of* |
| *horseradish sauce* | *horseradish sauce* |
| *2 × 15 ml spoons single* | *2 tablespoons single* |
| *cream* | *cream* |

Preparation time: 15 minutes
Cooking time: 1½–2 hours (or 25 minutes using a pressure cooker)

Wash the beetroot well but do not peel or trim away anything other than the leaves. Put into a pan of boiling, salted water, cover and simmer for 1½–2 hours until tender, depending on size.
Alternatively, put the beetroot in a pressure cooker, and cook them following the manufacturer's instructions.
Drain the beetroot, peel off the skins, then cut each one into 1 cm/½ inch dice, place in a serving dish and keep warm.
Melt the butter or margarine in a saucepan over a low heat, then blend in the flour. Remove the pan from the heat and gradually stir in the milk. Bring to the boil and add the grated rind and juice of the orange, the horseradish sauce and the cream. Taste and adjust the seasoning, pour the sauce over the beetroot and sprinkle over the parsley. Serve hot with a main course such as grilled mackerel.

Brussels sprouts with chestnuts; Beetroot with orange and horseradish sauce; Baked pepper and onion; Caramelized onions

# Baked pepper and onion

**Metric**
50 g butter
225 g onions, peeled and
    thinly sliced
1 red pepper, cored, seeded
    and finely sliced
1 green pepper, cored,
    seeded and finely
    sliced
few sprigs of fresh thyme
1 × 2.5 ml spoon dried
    thyme
freshly ground black
    pepper

**Imperial**
2 oz butter
8 oz onions, peeled and
    thinly sliced
1 red pepper, cored, seeded
    and finely sliced
1 green pepper, cored,
    seeded and finely
    sliced
few sprigs of fresh thyme
½ teaspoon dried
    thyme
freshly ground black
    pepper

Preparation time: 10 minutes
Cooking time: 50 minutes
Oven: 180°C, 350°F, Gas Mark 4

Put the butter into an ovenproof dish, cover and place in the oven to melt. Stir in the onions, peppers, thyme, salt and pepper. Cover the dish, return it to the oven and cook for about 45 minutes until tender. Serve with roast lamb or chicken.

# Caramelized onions

**Metric**
450 g small onions
salt
25 g sugar
2 × 15 ml spoons water
25 g butter
a little rock salt

**Imperial**
1 lb small onions
salt
1 oz sugar
2 tablespoons water
1 oz butter
a little rock salt

Preparation time: 10 minutes
Cooking time: 20 minutes

Boil the onions in their skins in salted water for 10–15 minutes or until tender. Drain, rinse under cold water, then remove the skins.
Meanwhile, put the sugar and water in a small saucepan and place over a low heat. When all the sugar has completely melted, bring the syrup to the boil, then boil rapidly for 5–10 minutes until it turns a light, golden brown.
Remove the pan from the heat and immediately add the onions and butter. Toss the onions in the sauce until they are evenly coated, then serve sprinkled with rock salt. Serve with roast beef or pork.

# Citrus potatoes

**Metric**
1 kg potatoes, peeled and
    cut into 1 cm chunks
salt
50 g butter
1 onion, peeled and
    finely chopped
grated rind and juice
    of 1 lemon
2 × 15 ml spoons chopped
    fresh chives

**Imperial**
2 lb potatoes, peeled and
    cut into ½ inch chunks
salt
1½ oz butter
1 onion, peeled and
    finely chopped
grated rind and juice
    of 1 lemon
2 teaspoons chopped
    fresh chives

Preparation time: 15 minutes
Cooking time: 1 hour 10 minutes
Oven: 190°C, 375°F, Gas Mark 5

Cook the potatoes in boiling, salted water for 5 minutes. Drain and leave them on one side.
Melt the butter in a saucepan. Add the chopped onion and fry until soft but not brown. Mix in the lemon rind and juice, then add the potatoes and shake the ingredients together. Turn the mixture into an oven-proof dish or roasting tin and cook in a preheated oven for about 1 hour until crisp and tender. Sprinkle with the chopped chives before serving with pork or bacon.

# Patates rösti

**Metric**
1 kg even-sized potatoes
salt
freshly ground black
    pepper
75 g butter

**Imperial**
2 lb even-sized potatoes
salt
freshly ground black
    pepper
3 oz butter

Preparation time: 10 minutes
Cooking time: 40 minutes

Cook the potatoes, still in their skins, in boiling, salted water for 10 minutes. Drain, rinse in cold water, then peel off the skins. Coarsely grate the potatoes into a bowl, then mix in salt and pepper.
Heat the butter in a 20 cm/8 inch frying pan. Add the grated potato and stir until all the butter has been thoroughly absorbed. Press the mixture down so that it forms a solid mass and cook slowly for about 30 minutes, moving the pan over the heat from time to time so that the potato browns evenly.
Invert the potato cake on to a plate and serve cut into wedges. Serve with cold meats or casseroles.
Serves 4–6

# Rumbledethumps

**Metric**
450 g potatoes, peeled,
    cooked and mashed
450 g cabbage, shredded
    and cooked
salt
freshly ground black
    pepper
50 g butter
4 spring onions, finely
    chopped

**Imperial**
1 lb potatoes, peeled,
    cooked and mashed
1 lb cabbage, shredded
    and cooked
salt
freshly ground black
    pepper
2 oz butter
4 spring onions, finely
    chopped

Preparation time: 35 minutes

This delicious Scottish border recipe is similar to the
English bubble and squeak and is especially good with
cold meats.

Mix the mashed potatoes and cooked cabbage together. Beat in the butter with plenty of salt and
pepper, then stir in the onions and turn the mixture
into a serving dish.

# Pommes mornay

**Metric**
750 kg potatoes, peeled
    and cut into 2.5 cm
    chunks
25 g butter or margarine
25 g plain flour
450 ml milk
100 g Cheddar cheese,
    grated
1/2 × 5 ml spoon mustard
    powder
pinch of cayenne
salt
freshly ground black
    pepper

**Imperial**
1 1/2 lb potatoes, peeled
    and cut into 1 inch
    chunks
1 oz butter or margarine
1 oz plain flour
3/4 pint milk
4 oz Cheddar cheese,
    grated
1/2 teaspoon mustard
    powder
pinch of cayenne
salt
freshly ground black
    pepper

Preparation time: 15 minutes
Cooking time: 25 minutes

Cook the potatoes in boiling, salted water for about 15
minutes until tender. Drain well.
Melt the butter or margarine in a pan, stir in the flour,
then gradually blend in the milk to make a smooth
sauce. Stirring all the time, bring the sauce to the boil
and cook for 2–3 minutes. Stir in three-quarters of the
cheese and add the mustard, cayenne, salt and pepper.
Turn the potatoes into a serving dish, pour over the
sauce and sprinkle the remaining cheese over the
surface. Place under a preheated hot grill until brown.

Citrus potatoes; Patates rösti; Rumbledethumps; Pommes mornay

# Creamy cucumber

| Metric | Imperial |
|---|---|
| 1 large cucumber, cut into 1 cm pieces | 1 large cucumber, cut into ½ inch pieces |
| salt | salt |
| 150 ml soured cream | ¼ pint soured cream |
| 1 × 15 ml spoon fresh sage, chopped | 1 tablespoon fresh sage, chopped |
| 1 × 15 ml spoon chopped fresh chives | 1 tablespoon chopped fresh chives |
| freshly ground black pepper | freshly ground black pepper |

Preparation time: 5 minutes
Cooking time: 15–20 minutes

Place the cucumber pieces in a steamer, sprinkle with salt and cook for 15–20 minutes until just tender. Turn the cucumber into a saucepan.

Mix the soured cream with the sage and chives, add salt and pepper to taste then add to the cucumber. Stir over a very low heat until thoroughly heated through. Delicious served with baked or grilled fish.
Serves 3–4

# Celery with orange and walnut

| Metric | Imperial |
|---|---|
| 2 small heads celery | 2 small heads celery |
| 2 large oranges | 2 large oranges |
| 50 g walnuts, roughly chopped | 2 oz walnuts, roughly chopped |
| 15 g butter | ½ oz butter |
| salt | salt |
| freshly ground black pepper | freshly ground black pepper |

# Broccoli à la polonaise

| Metric | Imperial |
|---|---|
| 750 g broccoli spears | 1½ lb broccoli spears |
| 50 g butter | 2 oz butter |
| 50 g fresh white bread-crumbs | 2 oz fresh white bread-crumbs |
| 1 hard-boiled egg, yolk sieved, white chopped | 1 hard-boiled egg, yolk sieved, white chopped |
| 1 × 15 ml spoon chopped fresh parsley | 1 tablespoon chopped fresh parsley |
| salt | salt |
| freshly ground black pepper | freshly ground black pepper |

Preparation time: 10 minutes
Cooking time: 15 minutes

The polonaise topping can also be served with asparagus or cauliflower.

Cut the larger pieces of broccoli in half if necessary. Cook the broccoli in boiling salted water for about 10 minutes or until just tender. Drain well.
Meanwhile, melt the butter in a saucepan, add the breadcrumbs and, stirring frequently, cook until brown. Stir in the sieved and chopped egg, parsley, salt and pepper. Arrange the broccoli spears in a warm serving dish and scatter the topping over the surface.
Serves 4–6

Preparation time: 10 minutes
Cooking time: 50 minutes
Oven: 180°C, 350°F, Gas Mark 4

Wash and trim the celery and cut each stick into 4–5 cm/1½–2 inch lengths. Using a potato peeler, thinly pare the rind from one of the oranges and shred it finely. Squeeze the juice from both the oranges.

Put the celery, walnuts and orange rind into an ovenproof dish and pour over the orange juice. Dot the butter over the surface and sprinkle generously with salt and pepper. Cover and cook in a preheated oven for 50 minutes or until the celery is tender. Serve with roast beef.
Serves 6

Creamy cucumber; Broccoli à la polonaise; Celery with orange and walnuts

# EXOTIC VEGETABLES

It is fascinating how the vegetable scene is continually changing. Up until only a few years ago, such vegetables as aubergine, courgette and pepper would have been considered exotic but today they can be found in many shops around the country. However, the larger stores and many of the Asian shops that are springing up in our big cities now display vegetables from further afield and here are just a few that you may find interesting to try.

## Chilli

Beware of using chillis in cookery as they are very fiery. They are red or green in colour and have a very glossy surface. In appearance, they resemble a small carrot.

It is the seeds of the chillis that are the hottest part so often they are removed. When preparing them for cooking, it is advisable to wear gloves as some very hot chillis, when they come into contact with the skin, can leave a tingling sensation which goes on for hours. Remember also not to put your hands near your eyes as this would cause similar discomfort. Cut off the stalk, split the chilli in half down the length, then carefully discard all the seeds. Chop or grind the flesh to use for cooking.

## Kohlrabi

Known as the 'turnip cabbage', kohlrabi is round like a turnip but with shoots emerging from the sides and bottom, not the top. It has either red or greenish-white skin and comes into the shops about July. It can be cooked, as a turnip, peeled and quartered and boiled in salted water for 30–40 minutes, then tossed in butter or coated with a white or cheese sauce. Often the leaves are also cooked like spinach for about 10 minutes, then

drained, chopped and tossed in butter to be used as a garnish around the edge of a dish of the boiled kohlrabi root. The more unusual and delicious way of serving them is in a salad (see recipe). Allow 100–175 g/4–6 oz per person served hot and 50–100 g/2–4 oz served cold as part of a salad.

## Mangetout

A member of the pea family, mangetout is a flat pea pod, bright green in colour and quite smooth. The peas are sometimes just detectable through the pod but as the pod has no parchment lining, they are eaten seed, pod and all. Available during the summer, they weigh very little so you will need only about 50 g/2 oz per person. Prepare by topping and tailing, then cook in a little boiling, salted water for 5–10 minutes. They should still be slightly crisp when served. Tossed in melted butter, they are delicious with roast lamb or duck.

## Müli

This unusual vegetable, found mainly in Asian stores, is sometimes called the 'Indian radish' mainly because its taste and texture is very similar to our own radish. However, it is totally different in appearance. Müli is a long, white, root vegetable similar in shape to a carrot but much bigger – 1 müli weighs about 450 g/1 lb. The vegetable is peeled, then can be grated to add to salad or cut into cubes to add to casserole dishes and curries. Allow 100–150 g/4–5 oz per person.

## Okra

Also known as 'ladies fingers', supposedly because the vegetable can be eaten, just like asparagus, in the fingers. Okra is light green in colour with almost a fur-like skin. It is about 10 cm/5 inches in length with 5 sides and white seeds inside. Trim off the top and tail. Then, either cook alone or add to stews, curries or soups. To cook, prepare the okra, put into a pan with

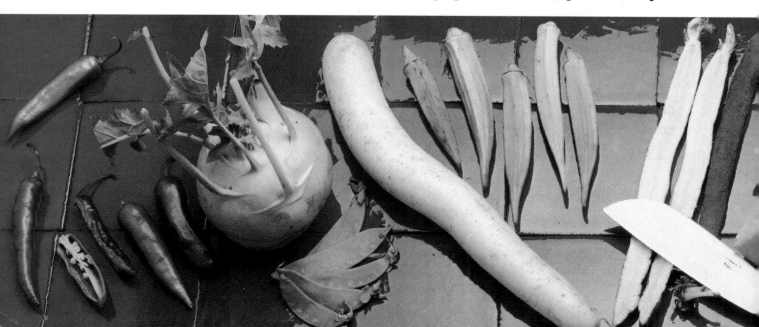

enough water to cover, then bring to the boil, cover and simmer for 5 minutes. Drain, melt 25–50 g/1–2 oz butter in the pan, add the okra and cook, covered, for a further 10–15 minutes until tender. Season, then serve with either the remaining butter in the pan or a home-made Hollandaise Sauce (see page 15). Allow 100 g/4 oz per person.

## Salsify

Also known as the 'oyster plant' or 'vegetable oyster', salsify is available in two varieties. One is white (salsify) and the other black (scorzonera). They are both very long and slender in shape. The vegetable is available during the winter months and is usually stored in sand or peat until required. When it starts to grow again in the spring, the green shoots that appear are sometimes cut and cooked as for asparagus or, alternatively, they are earthed up to be blanched in the same way as for chicory.

Never peel the vegetable as it will lose its flavour. Scrape, cut into 5 cm/2 inch lengths and keep in cold water with a little added lemon juice until required. Cook in boiling, salted water with a little vinegar for about 30 minutes. Drain and then serve tossed in butter or coated in a white sauce. Scorzonera bleeds a lot when prepared so it is advisable to just scrub it thoroughly to remove all the dirt then cook, whole, in boiling, salted water for about 40 minutes or until tender. Trim the ends, rub off the skin and serve as for salsify. Allow 175 g/6 oz per person.

## Spaghetti marrow

A member of the squash family, spaghetti marrows are bright yellow in colour and about 23 cm/9 inches in length. The flesh, once cooked, comes away from the skin in long, spaghetti-like strands.

To cook, boil the vegetable whole in salted water for about 30 minutes. Cut in half, remove the seeds and scoop out the flesh, toss in butter and serve as an accompanying vegetable. Spaghetti marrow can also be left to cool then served as part of a salad, tossed in a well-flavoured dressing.

## Squash

The squash family is very large, covering a vast selection of vegetables. It can be divided into two main categories; summer squash – marrows, winter squash – pumpkins. The pumpkin is large and round, coming in various shades of orange. The flesh and seeds resemble a marrow although the flesh is normally bright orange in colour. Pumpkins can be boiled, steamed, baked and puréed. They are also added to pies, stews, chutneys and jams. Buy the flesh by the ½ kg/1 lb. Peel off the skin, remove the seeds, cut into pieces, then boil in salted water for about 10–15 minutes until soft. Toss in butter and serve, or mash and mix with grated nutmeg. Allow about 175 g/6 oz squash per person.

## Sweet potatoes

These have a reddish skin and orange flesh. They were the first type of potato to be introduced into Britain and are found widely on the American continent. As the name suggests, they have a sweet taste and can be peeled and boiled or roasted like a normal potato. They are also interchangeable with yams. Allow 100–175 g/4–6 oz per person.

## Yams

A member of the root family, yams are long in shape and about 8 cm/3 inches in diameter. They are sold by the 450 g/1 lb and have a milky white flesh and greyish-brown skin. Yams, like sweet potatoes, can be boiled or roasted. They are also very good added to casseroles. Allow 100–175 g/4–6 oz per person.

# Kohlrabi salad

**Metric**
350 g kohlrabi, peeled and grated
1 green pepper, cored, seeded and chopped
2 sticks celery, cleaned and chopped
25 g seedless raisins
about 4 × 15 ml spoons cooking oil
2 thick slices white bread, crusts removed, cut into 1 cm cubes

**Dressing:**
1 × 15 ml spoon malt vinegar
3 × 15 ml spoons oil
1 × 15 ml spoon crunchy peanut butter
1 × 15 ml spoon tomato ketchup
salt
freshly ground black pepper

**Imperial**
12 oz kohlrabi, peeled and grated
1 green pepper, cored, seeded and chopped
2 sticks celery, cleaned and chopped
1 oz seedless raisins
about 4 tablespoons cooking oil
2 thick slices white bread, crusts removed, cut into 1/2 inch cubes

**Dressing:**
1 tablespoon malt vinegar
3 tablespoons oil
1 tablespoon crunchy peanut butter
1 tablespoon tomato ketchup
salt
freshly ground black pepper

Preparation time: 10 minutes

Put the kohlrabi, pepper, celery and raisins into a bowl and mix them all together.
Heat the oil in a frying pan and fry the bread cubes until crisp, to make croûtons. Drain them on kitchen paper and leave on one side.
Put the vinegar, oil, peanut butter and tomato ketchup into a jar with plenty of salt and pepper. Cover and shake vigorously until all the ingredients have emulsified. Pour the dressing over the salad and toss it well. Just before serving, mix in a few of the croûtons and sprinkle the rest over the top.
Serves 3–4

Stir-fried mangetout; Kohlrabi salad; Salsify in buttery herb sauce

# Stir-fried mangetout

**Metric**
225 g mangetout, topped and tailed
1 large red pepper, cored, seeded and thinly sliced
2 × 15 ml spoons oil
1 × 15 ml spoon soy sauce
salt
freshly ground black pepper

**Imperial**
8 oz mangetout, topped and tailed
1 large red pepper, cored, seeded and thinly sliced
2 tablespoons oil
1 tablespoon soy sauce
salt
freshly ground black pepper

Preparation time: 5 minutes
Cooking time: 5–10 minutes

Mix the mangetout with the pepper. Heat the oil in a large frying pan or wok. Add the vegetables and, stirring all the time, cook them over a medium heat until they start to soften. Mix in the soy sauce, salt and pepper, then cook for a further 2–3 minutes. Serve with grilled meat such as pork chops.

# Salsify in buttery herb sauce

**Metric**
750 g salsify, scraped
a little vinegar
salt
50 g butter
1 1/2 × 15 ml spoons chopped fresh mixed herbs (thyme, sage, marjoram, parsley)

**Imperial**
1 1/2 lb salsify, scraped
a little vinegar
salt
2 oz butter
1 1/2 tablespoons chopped fresh mixed herbs (thyme, sage, marjoram, parsley)

Preparation time: 10 minutes
Cooking time: 40 minutes

Put the salsify in boiling salted water, add a little vinegar and cook for about 30 minutes until tender. Drain thoroughly.
Melt the butter in the pan, return the salsify to it, cover and cook over a high heat, shaking the pan often, until the salsify starts to brown. Sprinkle over the herbs with extra salt. Turn into a serving dish. This is particularly delicious served with roast beef.

# Chilli and tomato sauce

| Metric | Imperial |
|---|---|
| 3 chillis, 2 seeded and 1 chopped | 3 chillis, 2 seeded and 1 chopped |
| 1 × 15 ml spoon oil | 1 tablespoon oil |
| 1 medium onion, peeled and chopped | 1 medium onion, peeled and chopped |
| 2 garlic cloves, peeled | 2 garlic cloves, peeled |
| 25 cm piece fresh ginger, peeled and chopped | 1 inch piece fresh ginger, peeled and chopped |
| 1½ × 5 ml spoons garam masala | 1½ teaspoons garam masala |
| 1 × 5 ml spoon cumin seeds | 1 teaspoon cumin seeds |
| 225 g tomatoes, peeled and chopped | 8 oz tomatoes, peeled and chopped |
| 150 ml beef stock | ¼ pint beef stock |
| salt | salt |

Preparation time: 15 minutes
Cooking time: 20 minutes

Chillis can be very hot, so it is wise to use them cautiously.

Chop the chillis, keeping the seeds of one of them and discarding the rest. Heat the oil in a saucepan, add the onion and fry gently until beginning to soften. Put the garlic cloves, chillis and ginger into a liquidizer and grind them together. Add the ground mixture, garam masala and cumin seeds to the onions in the pan. Stir, then add the tomatoes and stock.
Bring the sauce to the boil, reduce the heat, cover and simmer for 15 minutes so that all the flavours combine. Serve with rice, spaghetti or hamburgers.

# Pumpkin omelette

| Metric | Imperial |
|---|---|
| 350 g pumpkin, peeled | 12 oz pumpkin, peeled |
| 4 eggs (size 2) | 4 eggs (size 2) |
| 25 g butter | 1 oz butter |
| 1 × 5 ml spoon chopped fresh sage | 1 teaspoon chopped fresh sage |
| salt | salt |
| freshly ground black pepper | freshly ground black pepper |

# Okra sauté

| Metric | Imperial |
|---|---|
| 2 × 15 ml spoons oil | 2 tablespoons oil |
| 1 medium onion, peeled and chopped | 1 medium onion, peeled and chopped |
| 450 g okra, washed, trimmed and cut into small pieces | 1 lb okra, washed, trimmed and cut into small pieces |
| 1 × 5 ml spoon ground coriander | 1 teaspoon ground coriander |
| 1 × 2.5 ml spoon chilli powder | ½ teaspoon chilli powder |
| salt | salt |
| 1 × 5 ml spoon garam masala | 1 teaspoon garam masala |
| 1 × 15 ml spoon lemon juice | 1 tablespoon lemon juice |

Preparation time: 10 minutes
Cooking time: 10–15 minutes

Heat the oil in a frying pan. Add the onion and fry gently until beginning to soften. Stir in the okra, coriander, chilli powder and salt. Cover and cook for 10–15 minutes over a low heat until tender. Sprinkle with the garam masala and lemon juice. Mix well and serve with plain boiled rice or as an accompaniment to curry or grilled meat.

Preparation time: 5 minutes
Cooking time: 10 minutes

Add the pumpkin to boiling salted water and cook for 10–15 minutes until soft. Drain well, then liquidize to a purée. Break the eggs into a bowl and beat together with the pumpkin, sage, salt and pepper.
Heat the butter in an omelette pan. Add the mixture and, over a high heat, stir it slowly as it starts to set. When brown underneath, fold the omelette in half and cook for a few minutes. Then turn on to a plate and serve immediately with a salad.
Serves 2 as a supper dish

# Spaghetti marrow with creole sauce

*Metric*
*1 small spaghetti marrow*

*Sauce:*
*450 g ripe tomatoes,*
  *peeled and chopped*
*25 g butter or margarine*
*1 medium onion, peeled*
  *and finely chopped*
*1 medium green pepper,*
  *cored, seeded and*
  *chopped*
*2 garlic cloves, crushed*
*1 bay leaf*
*1 × 10 ml spoon plain*
  *flour*
*150 ml vegetable or beef*
  *stock*
*salt*
*freshly ground black*
  *pepper*

*Imperial*
*1 small spaghetti marrow*

*Sauce:*
*1 lb ripe tomatoes,*
  *peeled and chopped*
*1 oz butter or margarine*
*1 medium onion, peeled*
  *and finely chopped*
*1 medium green pepper,*
  *cored, seeded and*
  *chopped*
*2 garlic cloves, crushed*
*1 bay leaf*
*1 dessertspoon plain*
  *flour*
*¼ pint vegetable or beef*
  *stock*
*salt*
*freshly ground black*
  *pepper*

Preparation time: 15 minutes
Cooking time: 30 minutes

Melt the butter or margarine in a saucepan. Add the onion and pepper and fry gently for a few minutes until beginning to soften. Stir in the garlic, tomatoes, bay leaf, flour and stock and bring slowly to the boil. Reduce the heat and simmer uncovered for about 20 minutes or until it is of a good consistency. Add salt and pepper to taste.

Meanwhile, boil the spaghetti marrow in salted water for about 30 minutes. Drain and cut the marrow in half. Remove the seeds, spoon in a little sauce and serve the rest separately. Alternatively, scoop out the marrow flesh into a warm serving dish and pour on the sauce.

Serves 2 as a first course

Chilli and tomato sauce; Pumpkin omelette; Okra sauté; Spaghetti marrow with creole sauce

# Candied sweet potatoes

| Metric | Imperial |
|---|---|
| 450 g sweet potatoes | 1 lb sweet potatoes |
| 225 g cooking apples, peeled and thickly sliced | 8 oz cooking apples, peeled and thickly sliced |
| 100 g light soft brown sugar | 4 oz light soft brown sugar |
| grated rind and juice of 1 orange | grated rind and juice of 1 orange |
| 1 × 5 ml spoon mixed spice | 1 teaspoon mixed spice |
| 25 g butter | 1 oz butter |
| 2 × 15 ml spoons sherry | 2 tablespoons sherry |
| salt | salt |

Preparation time: 10 minutes
Cooking time: 1 hour 30 minutes
Oven: 180°C, 350°F, Gas Mark 4

Scrub the potatoes, then boil in their skins in salted water for 30 minutes until tender. Drain and when cold enough to handle, peel off the skins. Cut the flesh in 2.5 cm/1 inch chunks. Mix it with the apple and put into a 1 litre/1½ pint dish.

Put the sugar, orange juice and rind, mixed spice, butter, sherry and salt into a saucepan and stir over a low heat until they are combined and the sugar has melted. Pour the liquid over the potatoes, then toss them lightly until evenly coated. Cook uncovered in a preheated oven for 1 hour, stirring occasionally so that potatoes absorb the liquid and brown slightly. Serve with baked ham or chicken.

# Baked spiced yam

| Metric | Imperial |
|---|---|
| 50 g butter | 2 oz butter |
| 2 eggs (size 2) | 2 eggs (size 2) |
| 50 g caster sugar | 2 oz caster sugar |
| pinch of ground allspice | pinch of ground allspice |
| salt | salt |
| freshly ground black pepper | freshly ground black pepper |
| 300 ml milk | ½ pint milk |
| 450 g yams, peeled and grated | 1 lb yams, peeled and grated |
| chopped fresh parsley, to garnish | chopped fresh parsley, to garnish |

Preparation time: 10 minutes
Cooking time: 1 hour
Oven: 180°C, 350°F, Gas Mark 4

Grease a 1.2 litre/2 pint shallow ovenproof dish with half the butter.

Beat the eggs and sugar together. Add the allspice, salt, pepper and milk. Stir in the grated yam, then pour the mixture into the dish. Dot the rest of the butter over the surface and cook uncovered in a preheated oven until golden brown and slightly risen. Garnish with parsley before serving as an accompaniment to pork or chicken.

# Eastern müli

| Metric | Imperial |
|---|---|
| 450 g müli | 1 lb müli |
| 1 × 15 ml spoon oil | 1 tablespoon oil |
| 1 onion, peeled and sliced | 1 onion, peeled and sliced |
| 2 × 15 ml spoons chopped fresh mint | 2 tablespoons chopped fresh mint |
| 1 × 5 ml spoon ground turmeric | 1 teaspoon ground turmeric |
| salt | salt |
| 1 × 1.25 ml spoon chilli powder | ¼ teaspoon chilli powder |
| 3 × 15 ml spoons hot water | 3 tablespoons hot water |
| 1 × 5 ml spoon garam masala | 1 teaspoon garam masala |
| 1 × 15 ml spoon lemon juice | 1 tablespoon lemon juice |

Preparation time: 10 minutes
Cooking time: 40 minutes

Trim and peel the müli and cut it into 2.5 cm/1 inch pieces. Heat the oil in a frying pan. Add the onion and fry gently until beginning to soften. Add the mint, turmeric, chilli powder and salt, then stir in the müli so it is well covered. Add the water, cover, shaking the pan occasionally, for 20 minutes.

Sprinkle with the garam masala and lemon juice. Replace the lid and cook for a further 10 minutes or until the müli is tender. Serve with rice or chappatis, or as an accompanying vegetable to curry when it will serve 4–6.
Serves 3

Eastern müli; Candied sweet potatoes; Baked spiced yam

# Index